Rock On, Tommy!

Rock On, Tommy!

CANNON AND BALL

WITH CHRIS GIDNEY

HarperCollins*Publishers*

HarperCollins*Publishers*
77–85 Fulham Palace Road, London W6 8JB
www.**fire**and**water**.com

First published in Great Britain in 2000
by HarperCollins*Publishers*
This edition 2001

3 5 7 9 10 8 6 4

Copyright © 2000 Bobby Ball and Tommy Cannon

Bobby Ball and Tommy Cannon assert the moral right
to be identified as the authors of this work

A catalogue record for this book
is available from the British Library

ISBN 0 00 711336 6

Printed and bound in Great Britain by
Omnia Books Ltd, Glasgow

Bobby and Tommy would like to dedicate this book to their families, who have been a source of great support throughout the good times and the bad.

Tommy is proud to have his grandchildren, Ben, Alex and Matthew, and his daughters Janette and Julie. Kelly, Zoe and Luke are his latest shining editions, which he admits would not have been possible without his wonderful wife, Hazel.

Bobby's grandchildren, Ben, Christian, Samuel, Robert, Jack and Bethany, are a constant delight to him. Joanne, Robert and Darren are the sparks in his life, and at the 'top of the tree', his wife Yvonne means more to him than he can say.

ACKNOWLEDGEMENTS

Writing an autobiography is always a demanding task because it involves so many personal elements of someone's life. In this case, two lives are involved. Joint autobiographies are a rarity and require all the more effort, and the authors would like to thank their families and friends for the strong support they have shown during the writing of this book.

CONTENTS

PREFACE

The Lancashire town of Oldham sits proudly beside northeast Manchester and is a short drive from one of the country's premier seaside resorts, Blackpool. This popular destination, with its three-mile promenade, extensive stretches of beach, three piers and many theatres, clubs and bars, remains at the heart of show-business glitz. The Victorian centre still manages to attract more than a million visitors a year with an extensive season running from early spring and culminating in the famous Blackpool Illuminations every November. Its world-famous Pleasure Beach offers increasingly dangerous rides to those thrill-seekers eager to be terrorized by the latest white-knuckle experiences.

To me, the energy and excitement of Blackpool has always been synonymous with life in the entertainment business. The rise and fall of the roller coaster, the win and lose of the slot machines, the fun and fear of the ghost train, all seem to underline the unexpected twists and turns of many a show-business life – and none more so, I know, than Cannon and Ball. If any comedy duo's lot is akin to a Blackpool funfair, it is theirs. The fortunes won and lost and the dips and dives of fame have shocked, moulded and changed them into the men they are today. In fact, the character changes that have taken place over many years are so significant that many of their peers in the profession still find the contrast hard to accept.

I first met Bobby and Tommy when they still had the dubious reputation of being the nastiest people in the business. Some support acts were so afraid of them they would even refuse the work rather than face the destructive force it could bring into their lives. As this story unfolds, you will begin to see why. Loved by audiences and hated by critics, little did anyone know of the personal anguish and pain hidden beneath the laughter.

Never before has Britain's top comedy act been so honest in opening up the truth about their past and their rise to fame. I have made sure of it! As their friend for many years, I know and understand their private and show-business lives and realize that it is the failures as well as the successes which bring this fascinating tapestry together, giving the full picture at last.

So, please take your place, make sure your seatbelt is secure, and brace yourself to plunge into the thrilling world of Cannon and Ball.

Chris Gidney

CHAPTER ONE

TEDDY BOYS

The pain of 50 years ago came flooding back as Tommy drove slowly past his childhood haunts. The Rolls-Royce turned heads in the street, out of keeping with his surroundings, and yet it demonstrated how far he had come since 27 June 1938 when Thomas Derbyshire made his first public appearance. Yet, for all the success of recent years, he was still unable to comprehend the disturbing memories of earlier days.

As I stood in the hallway and watched my father walk slowly out of the door, little did I know that I would never see him again. Confused and frightened, I was just five years old. None of it made any sense to me, but I knew somewhere deep inside that it wasn't meant to be like this.

My emotions were tossed around like a boat in a storm, thrown between happiness and sadness. The source of my fear had now gone, but I still felt a great loss. At least I still had my mother, though my father's departure meant we were now totally alone. I don't think I understood the reasons why; all I knew was that my father wasn't there any more and I didn't have to contend with his fearful moods any longer.

My biological father was named Tom. He was a tall man, standing six foot one, and he worked down the coalmines in Durham. He met my mother and moved to Oldham. When the Second World War broke out in 1939 he joined the Army and worked his way up to Sergeant Major. A strange and complex man, I think he loved me, but he didn't show it in ways that I expected. An only child, I remember having most of everything material thrust upon me. He bought me a bicycle, a full-size toy car, and I had a train set that ran the whole length of my bedroom. Whilst all the other kids around me had to settle for having little or nothing in the way of toys, I had so many. I suppose it was his way of showing love, but material things don't make up for everything.

One day he would play with me and the next day he would give me a bashing around the head for nothing. I would sit terrified, waiting for the moment when he would return to the house, either before or after his diversion to the pub. Even when I was tucked up in bed I wasn't safe from his anger, which overflowed for no good reason. He must have been a deeply unhappy man, and his frustrations would often culminate in a beating for me. Alongside the emotional and physical bruising, the uncertainty of each day was soul destroying. I didn't know whether I was coming or going, whether today I was going to be loved or hated.

As adults we must stop for a moment and realize how the experiences of childhood affect us for the rest of our lives. We have to be so careful that we don't give our children extra baggage to carry through life, because they will have enough of their own. Memories are worn like an unwanted overcoat for the rest of our lives when adults force their problems onto their children without any thought of what damage is being caused. Looking back, I'm certain that my father didn't understand what insecurities he would leave me with. The devastating effect as I grew older was that I learned to shut out all the things that might hurt me. I became an expert at building walls and avoiding anything that caused distress.

The relief in our home when my father left was tangible. I thought my mother and I would be very happy on our own, but I hadn't realized how lonely she was for adult company. When I was about seven years of age my mother remarried, this time to a man named Eddie Hall. He was a lorry driver, and for some reason we took an instant dislike to one another. Over the years my dislike turned to hate. Not only had I acquired a new stepfather, but I had new stepbrothers and stepsisters to contend with too. Eddie had four children, Roy, Terry, Sheila and Marion. They had no mother to take care of them and had automatically been put into a home. When my mother married Eddie, though only standing four foot eleven but with a heart as big as the world, she decided to take his children out of the home and brought them to live with us as a family.

I don't think she realized what she had done as my whole world suddenly collapsed. I didn't know how to deal with the fact that I had been robbed of my stability once more. After being an only child, I was suddenly the member of a large family. I began to resent my mother for bringing these strange people into my life. She sat me down and tried to explain things and slowly, over a period of time, my resentment against her subsided a little. I hated my new stepfather, though, because he was the one who had come between my mother and me. I blamed him for taking away the security my mother gave and replacing it with something I hadn't chosen. I was angry because it seemed that my mother had turned her back on me for someone else. I was very resentful of everyone and very, very lonely.

My new brothers and sisters were very close, having been brought up together in a home, but I wasn't part of their intimacy. I was the one on the outside. I wasn't used to having siblings arguing and fighting like normal kids, and when they picked on me it was frightening. It certainly toughened me up, and I quickly saw that my only chance was to stand on my own two feet. It couldn't have been easy for my mother; she must have struggled in many ways. Taking care of a large family of seven must have been no easy feat. Although money was scarce, however, she had love in abundance, and it was her love that kept us all afloat.

Our home, No 1 Taylor Street, Oldham, was one of those terraced houses that seemed to be obligatory in the north of England. Today they are called 'town houses', but to me they are still just terraced houses and always will be. There were rows and rows of them in Oldham, all with a small yard and a passageway at the back, before starting again with another row of houses. Although uniform in appearance, it was a great place to grow up in, and a place of adventure. It was a time when people could leave their doors open and not be worried about being burgled. Children would run from one house to the next, then out though the back door and down the passage, only to reappear in another house down the street. This all happened while the wives gossiped as they cleaned their front steps. It was a ritual that their front steps had to be clean. 'She's a dirty bugger,' they would say if they saw a grubby front step.

As soon as I was allowed out of the house alone, I started to knock about with a bunch of kids who obviously weren't angels. We used to go around the neighbourhood doing the usual things that wild kids do, breaking into cars and stuff like that. The only reason I didn't end up in borstal was because I was too young. Some of the kids I grew up with inevitably turned into criminals in later life and I think I would have been one of them if we hadn't moved home when we did. I had just turned 14 and this proved to be the turning point in my young life.

Our move to a large council estate that overlooked Oldham was wonderful. Imagine my delight when we swapped our little terraced house for a three-bedroomed home with space all around us. The estate had a great community spirit, with lots of people from all walks of life pursuing different pastimes and interests. There were three or four football teams and cricket teams, so I was able to hide away amongst all this activity. A typical Sunday morning scene would be of women chatting over the fences with their young children playing around their feet, whilst the men and boys walked up the road with their football boots over their shoulders. It was a simple life then and it saddens me to see how much we have lost through that strange thing we call progress.

Within days of moving to the estate I made my first big mistake. There was a kid named Alan Chadwick who lived three houses away from us, and my stepbrother Terry told me that to be tough I had to be the first to fight him. He said this would prove that I was a force to be reckoned with. I had never been a lover of violence, but I thought that if that was how things were done on a council estate, so be it. I was very confident that my good physique would enable me to win, and the next time I saw Alan I told him I was going to beat him up.

'You're about to find out exactly who you're messing with!' I proudly announced. I posed, thrust my chest out, and stood there acting like a tough guy as best I could. After a moment's silence, with an incredulous look on his face, Alan reached out and hit me bang on the nose, then proceeded to give me the beating of my life. As I lay on the ground with blood running into my mouth, I vowed to be quicker next time!

Alan must have appreciated my efforts nonetheless, because we soon became friends. I was glad that I had achieved my original aim of being noticed as tough, albeit not quite as I'd planned. Violence soon seemed to be part of growing up. I was still intensely angry inside and expressed my frustrations physically. I was game for any fight, and I didn't need an audience. The ability to demonstrate my mettle was a great 'fix' by itself.

On one occasion a gang of us had been running around the estate with peashooters. Shooting dried peas at the windows of houses, we would then duck down behind a bush or a wall. As the occupants came out to investigate the noise, we would shoot peas at them and then run away. It was a great laugh. Then one man came out of his house and started to chase us. We split up and I was running as if my life depended on it. I turned a corner and ran slap-bang into the local policeman, nearly knocking him off his feet. He grabbed me and clipped me around the ear, then sent me home. By the time I arrived, my stepfather had somehow heard about the whole affair and proceeded to give me another bashing because, as he said, it was his job to punish me, not the policeman's.

The rebuke didn't make a lot of difference in persuading me to cease my aggressive pursuits, but luckily for me violence was relegated to a back shelf when I discovered the joys of football. Having played at school, my interest increased as time went by. I was accepted for one of the teams on the estate and we climbed quite high up in the amateur league. The game became my obsession and it was all I could think about. I wanted to be like one of my football heroes such as Sir Stanley Matthews, and I wasn't a bad player. I tried rugby once, but I dislocated my shoulder, so it was back to football. Later on in life I actually fulfilled one of my dreams by scoring a goal at Wembley. It was in a charity match before 60,000 people and there I was, playing football on that hallowed turf, and to top it all I scored a goal. Life is full of wonderful turns sometimes.

By contrast, Bobby's childhood had none of the fears and worries that Tommy had to endure, and in the sort of incredible twist usually reserved for a novel, Bobby was born at the same hospital as Tommy, only six years later. They would have to wait nearly 20 years before they met, destined to take a journey together through a life of incredible highs and abysmal lows. Robert was the only son of Bob and May Harper and made his grand entrance at the Boundary Park Hospital on 28 January 1944. He was the boy that his father had always wanted, and as they already had two daughters, Robert made the family complete in his father's eyes. Although extremely poor, what they lacked in riches they made up for with an abundance of love. Bobby lived the first few years of his life in a condemned building high on the moors overlooking the village of Shaw. Abject poverty didn't seem to bother the young boy, however, as Bobby describes how he quickly discovered that life was to be a great adventure.

ROCK ON, TOMMY!

I was so ugly as a child they put me in an incubator with tinted windows. My mother entered me into an ugly contest and the judges said 'no professionals'. Actually, I was called her 'blue baby', and as I got older my mother explained that I was born with a kind of eczema on my skin that formed a crust and made me look a very strange colour. The hospital apparently kept us in while they tried to get rid of it. The doctors tried many things but couldn't seem to solve the problem. Eventually my dad told the hospital that he was taking us home and that he was going to treat it himself. As he was about to leave an old nurse took him to one side and gave him some ointment. Why the hospital hadn't tried this before, my mother never told me, but when my father got us home he covered me in the greasy substance. After a few weeks the scabs on my skin came off and, in my mother's own words, 'Eeh, Robert, you had a beautiful olive skin underneath.'

Childhood was simply wonderful, even though I think my father must have been a hand-grenade instructor – every time he changed my nappy he pulled the safety pin out and threw me over the settee. We were poor, but to me it never seemed that way, except at Christmas when toys seemed to be a scarcity. I always wanted a cowboy outfit, but never got one. I got some guns and a holster, but never the suit. It didn't matter: with my two sisters Sylvia and Mavis, and a mother and father who loved me, I was pampered all the way. I knew my father was proud of me, but my mother mollycoddled me because I was the youngest. Mavis and Sylvia used to mother me too, so life for me was good in every way. The love that surrounded me somehow balanced the poverty we lived in.

Our home was in a small hamlet called Shaw. Today it's a suburb of Oldham, but in those days it was a village isolated by hills. Residents would never leave; there was no reason to explore beyond the streets that supplied everything they needed. There wasn't really any good public transport and nobody could afford a car. My mum would walk down to the shops each morning before work to buy the food for the evening meal.

Our house was condemned, which basically means that it was unfit to live in by normal standards, even in those days. For my sisters and me, however, it was an adventure playground. In our imaginations, derelict houses became castles and piles of waste and rubble were an Aladdin's treasure store just waiting to be explored.

Living conditions were cramped as the house had only a small living room and an even smaller kitchen. Upstairs consisted of one bedroom and a space at the top of the stairs. I slept in the bedroom with my mother and father, and my sisters slept on the landing. We had no curtains because the walls were so damp that whenever my mother tried to hang any the plaster just crumbled away. We did without. In any case, all we could see from the windows was moorland, so the only things that would be looking in through the window would be sheep.

The roof was a different matter. It was so bad that it couldn't even be repaired. It was considered so unstable that the landlord couldn't get a roofer to risk the danger of fixing it, so when it rained, it poured both inside and out. We had great fun trying to dodge the streams that would flood in through the gaping holes. In the winter it was always damp in our house, and it's a wonder we were always so healthy.

Bath night meant my mother boiling many pans of hot water, which she would pour into a metal tub in the kitchen. The tub would be hung on a hook outside, ready for use. Underneath the house was a huge cellar, and that was where the monsters of my imagination lived. One year the kitchen floor fell into the cellar and we had to use wooden planks to get into the front room. It only served to heighten my visions of the dark and scary trolls lurking beneath us. For all its faults, though, I loved that house, and spent some of the happiest times of my life there.

The living room had a huge black fireplace, normally only found in the kitchens of stately homes, and the hearth had huge ovens built into the side of it for slow-baking home-made bread. I remember the fireplace well, because it was here that my sisters and I would cuddle up close in one of the enormous ovens and listen to Mam telling us stories. It was a magical and wonderful time as we sat there, warm and secure. The gas lamp cast a strange light, and our young minds would wander wherever my mother's stories took us. At a certain time she would tell us to be quiet and listen, and we would sit there trying to catch some imaginary sound, when suddenly we would hear my father's clogs clattering as he came down the hill.

My father wore clogs all his life. In the thirties and forties most working-class people in the north of England wore them as they were hard wearing and lasted a very long time. They were very economical too, being made of hard leather fixed to a wooden sole, with pieces of rubber or iron nailed on the bottom so that the wooden sole wouldn't wear out. My father was very proud of his clogs and they would always be polished so that you could see your face in them. They were great for us kids too, because we always knew when he was coming.

When he saw us all sitting round the fireplace his face would light up and he would give each of us a kiss, finally hugging my mother and passing her a bottle of stout ale that he had bought from the pub. They were wonderful times and occasionally I wish I could travel back in some kind of time machine, just to be there once more.

My parents embraced each other with a genuine love that is rarely found and I was really blessed to have them. Both were very small, my father standing at just five foot and my mother at four foot eleven, but in their hearts they were giants. They were hard working too. My mother toiled from dawn till dusk at the cotton mill, and my father worked the same hours at a firm that made asbestos. The few hours they managed to spend with us were always precious. My dad worked as a drug weigher, having to assess all the different components that went into making asbestos. A skilled job in many ways, it would probably be considered quite dangerous these days.

My dad was a sportsman in his youth and this activity was important to him. As I was the only son he was so keen for me to follow in his footsteps, but sadly it was not to be. He would take me onto the common in front of the houses with either an old football or a cricket bat, and would spend hours trying to teach me and engender some interest. I would do my best, but deep in my heart I was just not interested and didn't feel comfortable with the competition of it all. The very act of it being thrust upon me probably robbed me of the opportunity to

11

discover a love of sport for myself. Sometimes I feel that I let my father down in this respect, but on the other hand I knew he was very proud of me in other ways.

My mother was a special lady, but then again, all mothers are, aren't they? She was only tiny and, looking back on old photographs, I remember that she was a beautiful-looking lady, with black hair and storytelling eyes that always promised a new secret waiting to be unearthed. My mother and father struggled through life, like a lot of people in those days. My mum's day would begin at 5.30 in the morning, when she got up to see my father off to work. After that she would get us up and dress us for 7.30, when we would all set off on the two-mile trek down to the nursery. This was attached to the cotton mill where my mother worked. She was a spinner and I remember that when she picked me up from the nursery after work she would always smell of cotton. It was a kind of a musty, warm, cosy smell, and I always associated it with my mother for years afterwards.

She arrived to pick us up at 5.30 promptly each afternoon, taking us home and preparing my father's tea. This was her way of life for many years, and my father worked just as hard. They never saw any rewards for their years of toil; they just took it as a normal way to live. They got on with it and enjoyed what they had without trying to gain what they couldn't. The simple things in life are often the best.

The greatest thing they did was to pass on their devotion, teaching me how to show love, how to hug, and how to reach out to other people. We never left the house without first kissing each other. They taught me how to pass love on to others, and that is one of the greatest gifts any of us can have. I took it all for granted at the time, but now I wish I had thanked them properly before they died.

Of my two sisters, I was closest to our Mavis – not because I liked her more, it was just an age factor. Sylvia was seven years older than I was, and our Mavis was only two years older, so I was naturally drawn to her. We used to play together and she became my best friend for life. Whenever I got into trouble our Mavis would be there, fighting my fights for me. She looked after me and we were like twins. Wherever our Mavis was, you could be sure to find me. To her I was 'our little Robert'. We would sing together in the house and put on little concerts for my mother and father. Our Sylvia never got involved in our concerts; she was too interested in boys.

It wasn't long before Mavis and I started to accompany our parents to the local working men's clubs at the weekends. They were wonderful places to us, as we would get up on the stage and sing for the people there. The lyrics for 'The Rich Maharaja From Magador' and 'Be My Girl' are still vivid in my mind. Our parents were proud of us and when we got up to sing my mother would sit there with her back straight and a kind of 'those are my children' look on her face. She wasn't a pushy woman; she was just proud of her offspring and was happy to see us enjoying ourselves. She would say that I got my talent from her side of the family, because her grandfather, Frank Williams, was a comic who used to work the pubs around Oldham in the 1920s.

She used to tell a funny story about Frank Williams. When I was a kid I used to turn my eyes into the corners to make a funny face, and my mother would shout at me. 'Stop that!' she would say. 'Your great-grandfather Frank used to do that and one day the wind changed and he stayed that way!' I didn't have a clue what she meant until I got older, but apparently he would turn his eyes in to get a comical reaction, and over the years the muscles in his eyes became weak and they eventually stayed put. I used to laugh when I thought about it. I imagined his billing: 'Frank Williams – the cross-eyed comic from Oldham'!

Despite my father's disappointment at my lack of sporting ability, he never made me feel bad, and I knew he would love me no matter what I was. Even though he loved my singing, he had no yearnings for me to go into show business because it was such an alien world. All my mum and dad knew was that everyone got a local job when they left school, got married, had kids and lived happily ever after. They were content for me just to survive in the world. They weren't ambitious people and passed these feelings on. I realized that it was good to have ambition, but it was obvious that my parents were happy with their lot. I was content with it too at the time.

Invitations for Mavis and myself to appear in local clubs increased. At the Higher Crompton Conservative Club one day, my father was unexpectedly approached by a stranger who offered to take me to London and manage a career for me. My father declined the offer, saying that he had waited a long time for a son and that he wasn't willing to let go of me so quickly.

I wasn't angry at this lost opportunity because I was too young to really understand what it meant, and if I had been my father I would have done exactly the same. Once again it proved that he loved me. I was quite happy to go to the different clubs every weekend with my mum and dad, and I don't know what would have happened if my father had agreed to the stranger's suggestion. Maybe my trip to London was not meant to be, for if I had gone, I wouldn't have met Tommy and there would have been no Cannon and Ball.

About six months after the meeting between my father and the stranger, the song 'He's Got The Whole World In His Hands' was released as a single by a 14-year-old boy named Laurie London. My father said that was the song the stranger had told him he wanted me to record. If I had recorded it my life would have been totally different from the way it is today. It's a strange thought.

Our Mavis and I continued singing around the clubs and it wasn't long before we became very popular around the area, with many people wanting to book us. It was around this time, when I was eight years old, that my parents received the news that they had been recommended for a council home. They were given a choice of two houses. One was on an estate surrounded by other houses and the other was in a row of houses with fields at the front and a cricket field at the back. Of course my father picked the one with the cricket field at the back.

We were all excited about moving to the new house and had been down into the village to see it, agreeing that it was quite wonderful. It had a front and back garden, three bedrooms, and even a bathroom. The day came for the move, but we couldn't afford to hire anyone to move us, so my parents decided to do it themselves. I can still see us now, looking like a Bedouin tribe, with all our belongings piled up on old prams and wheelbarrows, pushing them down from the hills to our new beginning.

We soon settled in with all the mod cons and I suddenly felt rich because we had running hot water and electricity. Having a bath became a luxury, and being able to read in bed late at night always caused shouts from Mam to 'Put that light out!'

The best thing of all was having my own bedroom. After years of having my mother and father sleeping across the room from me, I now had my own space. I even had a wardrobe of my own. Granted, it was pretty old at the time, but it was my own. I could do what I wanted in my bedroom – there was no one watching me. I could read, I could sit up in bed, I could even walk around the room in the middle of the night if I wanted and there was no one there to tell me, 'Go to sleep.' I think for the first few nights I never really got to sleep because I was so excited. Feeling very wealthy, I could now invite friends back from school and take them up to my own room. There were no interruptions and I had something that now belonged to just me.

The new home must have increased the general feelings of confidence for Mavis and me, because our performing career went from strength to strength and we started singing all over the north of England. My mother would accept the invitations and chaperone us, and my father would come too when work allowed. Travelling by train from place to place, we would then catch a cab from the station to the venue. My mother was a great tour manager.

We started doing 'warm-ups' for BBC Radio in Manchester. How we got the job I can't remember, but I think someone saw us performing and put us forward for it. Our Mavis and I would sing for the radio audience and hopefully, with us looking like little angels, this would put the audience in a good mood for whatever programme they were going to see. Never work with animals and children, they say!

We also did such 'spots' for many famous shows, including *The Comedy Bandbox*, *The Jimmy Clitheroe Show* and many others. Our fee was £3, which wasn't a huge amount once all the expenses had been taken out for travelling and digs. What was left went towards helping the family. It was while we were doing the warm-up for *The Comedy Bandbox* one day that the star of the show came walking down the corridor. Ronnie Hilton was a huge name in the fifties and had enjoyed many hit records. We had finished our act and were waiting to go home when he came up and said that he had enjoyed us very much, and he gave me an apple. I met Ronnie many years later when Tommy and I were performing at the London Palladium and I mentioned it to him, but alas, he didn't remember. I did, and I kept that apple for a long time until my mother had to throw it away for health reasons.

When Mavis and I got a booking for two weeks at the Majestic Hotel on the Isle of Man, it was wonderful because it doubled as a family holiday. Mam and Dad acted the proud parents whilst my sisters and I had such fun on the beach in the sunshine every day. It didn't seem like work at all and I thought, 'If this is what show biz is all about, then sign me up!'

By the time I was 12, rock'n'roll had become the latest craze and our Mavis and I got booked to appear at the old Empire Theatre in Oldham. The show contained some of the best British rock'n'roll acts around. Topping the bill was a guy named Terry Dene. He was the biggest draw in show business in those days. Looking like an early Cliff Richard, he sported a mock 'Elvis' haircut, sideburns and tight pants. Girls would mob the stage just to try to touch him. I think he was one of the first rock-'n'roll rebels. He once got drunk and smashed up a hotel room, and the police came and arrested him. The next day his misdemeanour was all over the front pages of the national papers. That night he went on stage drinking a glass of milk as a demonstration of his sobriety. He seemed a likable rebel and the people just loved him. A few years later he told the public that he had become a Christian, and I noticed how he was dropped like a hot potato. He just seemed to disappear from public view. Maybe everybody thought he would preach at his gigs instead of singing!

Also on the bill at the Empire was a crazy guy named Wee Willie Harris. He dyed his hair different colours every week – one week it would be bright green and the next bright orange. This was about 20 years before punks thought it was a new idea. Arriving on stage dressed in a leopardskin suit and with his mop of bright orange hair, he would run around screeching out rock-'n'roll numbers. He was a sight to behold!

Lower down the bill was a double act called The Most Brothers. They also dyed their hair, but unlike Wee Willie they only dyed it one colour, and that was platinum blond. This was at a time when only women dyed their hair, so it was quite a radical approach. They were the British equivalent of the Everly Brothers. One of them, Mickey Most, went on to become one of the most successful producers of the seventies and eighties. Many of the records we heard in the seventies were produced by him and released on his label, Rak Records.

Our Mavis and I were at the bottom of the bill. I think our names were smaller than the printers', but to us this was the big time. We were singing in our home town and appearing on the bill with all these great rock'n'roll artistes. It was like a dream come true. Here was I, a 12-year-old boy, standing backstage watching all the performers walking back and forth with their slicked-back hair and weird clothes. I was with guys who were rebels and idols in our eyes. It blew my mind away – so much so that not long afterwards I stopped singing our 'sweet little songs', because I wanted to be like them. I wanted to be a real 'teddy boy'.

Life on stage had become too predictable. I needed to be different. By the time I had reached 14 years of age, school had become a place just to pass time until I could leave at 15, get a job and become a 'real man'. What a foolish child I was. There was all this knowledge and teachers to teach it to me, and all I wanted to do was roam the streets with my friends, chatting up girls and longing for the day when I could leave school and get a dead-end job. I was to have many of those.

Every weekend I'd catch the bus with my mates and go the four miles or so into Oldham. By now I was dressing in drainpipe trousers and a long wool coat with velvet on the collar. I'd managed to save some of my pocket money from our gigs and from a newspaper round. I went down to Jackson's Tailors in Oldham and bought the suit I had been eyeing up for months. I was so proud. This was a real teddy boy outfit. My hair was combed to look like Tony Curtis (before he wore a wig) and I thought I looked fantastic. In truth I must have looked a right prat. What with wearing a long coat and being so small, I probably looked like one of Ken Dodd's Diddy Men.

It was on one of our weekend jaunts that I found myself at a place called The Green. It was really just a scrappy piece of spare ground in the middle of Oldham, but someone had the great idea of putting a fairground ride on it and it became a magnet for young people. It was here that I saw a girl I thought was particularly lovely. I stood near her, all four foot eleven of me, with my hair greased down with a ton of Brylcreem. My brothelcreepers made me look as if I was wearing orthopaedic shoes. But I looked at this girl, and thought she would instantly fancy me because, foolishly, I thought I looked terrific.

To my amazement she didn't even notice me, so I went right over to her. She turned out to be very friendly and told me her name was Helen Lavity. We arranged to see each other the following weekend. The days passed slowly as I waited for the weekend to arrive. Eventually it did and I made my way up to Oldham to see Helen. When I got there, she was nowhere to be found. I had been ditched. I searched for her, but couldn't find her anywhere.

As I was walking down a street I saw a girl with long red hair and asked her whether she knew Helen Lavity. She said she did, but she didn't know where Helen was. Not to be beaten, I decided to spend the rest of the afternoon talking to this girl with the long red hair. Her name was Joan Lynn. It's funny how life works, because she went on to be my first wife.

CHAPTER TWO

TEENAGER IN LOVE

Tommy's adolescent years contained a frustrating mixture of jobs and emotions. The increasing isolation created by his stepfamily resulted in serious insecurities which would affect Tommy for the rest of his life. Throughout the ever changing phases of youth, however, one thing remained constant: his love of sport. It is ironic that whilst Bobby's father was trying to encourage his son to show more interest in games, Tommy's stepfather was doing the complete opposite. Sport was the main drive in Tommy's life, though, and became his anchor when it seemed that his deep unhappiness might simply have swept him away.

I desperately wanted to be a professional footballer or cricketer, and would happily have given up everything to do that. I knew I had the talent for it, but I wasn't encouraged or pushed by my stepfather, which made me very sad. Even at school I showed an aptitude for it, captained both the cricket and football teams, and one year bowled out the whole team in a cricket match. I received a signed bat from the England cricket team as an award for my circuiting skills. I don't know where that bat eventually ended up, and looking back I don't think I understood the sentimental value it would have for me in later years. It was a great honour to play for the Old-ham Schoolboys because I was picked from hundreds of hopefuls in Oldham, but I didn't make it to the big leagues because I lacked confidence. Again, I blame my stepfather.

I left school and started on my journey of jobs, wan-dering from one place of employment to another. My first job was as a 'doffer' in the local cotton mill. My responsibility was to unload the full bobbins, replacing them with empty ones ready for the spinners to fill them with the wound yarn. It was a soul-destroying job, really. My next job was with a wholesale fruit and veg firm, and I even found myself down a coal pit for a month. That was really frightening, and I would get very claustrophobic during the four-hour stints between sur-facing for fresh air.

My stepfather wouldn't listen to my pleas to enter a trade. I always fancied being a plumber, but I wasn't given the opportunity because my stepbrother didn't finish his apprenticeship, which angered my stepfather. This resulted in a block on any of the other children doing an apprenticeship, ensuring that I became a labourer instead because it brought more immediate money into the home.

At the age of 17, I ended up working at the George Dews Construction Company, which was quite a culture shock for me because all the young boys who started work on those sites were seen as 'chief cook and bottle washer'. Treated like a little slave, I cooked breakfast in the morning for 150 men. They would bring in whatever they wanted for breakfast – some might bring in eggs and bacon, some might bring in sausages, some might bring just bread for toasting, but whatever it was, it had to be cooked. They would leave it on their benches in a shed where they would have their breakfast, and it was my job to prepare it. Boy, if I didn't have their breakfast ready in time or mixed up whose breakfast was whose, I was in big trouble. A smack around the head was the usual way of telling me I had got it wrong.

One day I took an old labourer a cup of tea and he was stood on his shovel looking around. 'Come here, son,' he said, looking over his shoulder. 'In this job, in order to dodge the foreman you have to have eyes in your bum.'

'What do you mean?' I asked, with all the naivety of a teenager. In reply he dropped his trousers, turned round and bent over, and there tattooed on each cheek of his backside was an eye. They weren't small either – the two eyes filled each cheek. He stood up and started laughing at my embarrassment. From that day, every time I saw him I could imagine these two huge eyes underneath his trousers winking at me.

At least I learnt some useful skills at George Dews. I started as a 'banksman', the name given to a machine operator, and ended up driving the bulldozers. Sitting amongst the controls of those enormous machines felt like a very powerful place to be, but there were days when I was so bored it was difficult to restrain myself from using the bulldozer to flatten anything that symbolized being trapped in this dead-end job.

The MRQ Construction Company was the next rung up the ladder. I was the only Englishman among 250 Irishmen. It was pretty rough. Some of them couldn't sign their name – they just put a cross on the paper when they collected their weekly wages. We would travel to each job in an old green truck, with a tarpaulin thrown over the top. The stench of men's pee in the back was horrendous and made me retch. Although the guys treated me well, they weren't the best of companions. The main drawback to the job, however, was that after a while I was the only teenager in Oldham with a Lancashire–Irish accent!

During all these many mini-careers I had a yearning to join the Forces. If I couldn't be a sportsman or have a trade, I would escape into the Army. After finally deciding that this was the life for me, I went down to the recruitment office. Standing in a long line of guys all wanting to be in the Army, I looked at each man and tried to guess his reason for signing up. Maybe some were there for adventures or the lure of foreign lands, and others because the Army seemed a better lifestyle than the one they had now. Waiting in the queue, I reflected that the latter was the reason I was there.

Suddenly I heard my name being bellowed by a tough-looking soldier in green. I was marched into a little booth and told to strip off. At that precise moment I thought about the eyes tattooed on the old labourer's backside, and wished that I could have borrowed them for a while, just to see the look on the doctor's face. I was confidence itself: compared to some of the other guys in line, I was well built with plenty of extra muscle. All my sporting activities had seen to that. The doctor gave me a medical, including the famous coughing routine, and everything seemed to work OK, but it was still embarrassing.

The medic, who had thick glasses and a white smock down to his knees, seemed pleased and I went home to wait eagerly for the arrival of my acceptance letter. I was so anxious that each day I was at the front door for half an hour waiting for the postman. As soon as the letter was in my hot little hands, I tore it open. Imagine my shock and disappointment when I read that I had been classed 'grade 3'. I was unfit for the Army! My heart sank. This couldn't be. There must be some mistake.

Scanning the letter quickly to find the reason for my rejection, I saw that I had been refused entry because of a perforated eardrum. I had played football and cricket for most of my young life, was at the peak of my physical fitness, and a perforated eardrum stopped me from realizing a life's ambition. It was one of the biggest disappointments of my life; but I suppose that if I had been accepted into the Forces my whole life would have been different. The only good thing about having a perforated eardrum was that later in life it probably saved me from listening to Bobby rattle on about one thing or another.

Aside from the disappointment of not getting into the Forces, life on the estate was pretty good. I now had a girlfriend called Olive, and we started to court with a vengeance. We would see each other every night and maybe go to the pictures, where we would indulge in passionate skirmishes in the back row. The rest of the week we sat in Olive's house with her mum and dad, who thought the world of me. In their eyes I was their future son-in-law, and in my eyes Olive was the girl I was going to marry. She lived just at the back of my house, so I could simply jump over my back fence and arrive in her garden. With four or five long steps I would be standing in her kitchen. I figured that she was a good bet because it saved me on the bus fares I'd had to pay to reach the previous loves of my life.

We went out for about 18 months and then Olive got a job babysitting three times a week. I didn't go with her because she said that the parents of the baby didn't want two young people in the house at the same time. I understood this and I was pleased that Olive was making extra money for herself. Our relationship seemed to suffer because we weren't seeing so much of each other, though. Olive seemed to be childminding all the time.

After about three weeks I asked her mum where Olive was babysitting. Her mother gave me directions and I decided to make Olive a surprise visit. When I reached the house where she was, for some strange reason I decided not to knock and just walked straight in. Olive was lying down on the settee in the front room, and on top was a guy kissing her passionately. They had obviously been drinking because all around the settee were beer bottles. I shouted and ran towards the guy to hit him. Suddenly he jumped up, grabbed a beer bottle and hit me over the head before disappearing out through the front door.

With beer and blood running down my face, the only thing I could think of to say was, 'You pig!' Needless to say, that was the end of Olive and me. Perhaps if I had been called Popeye, things might have been different. After that I gave up on girls and threw myself back into football. What I didn't realize then was that the rejection from Olive had such a big effect on me that I started to build even more walls around myself. It was a natural way to protect myself from being hurt again, but the problem was that I was a pretty good wall-builder. I built them so high and thick that they would stay put for much of my life, and it's only recently that I've started to take them down. Isolation is a deadly friend, yet it was really the only one I had. Feeling dejected and rejected, I retreated into my own world, becoming a loner.

Although I played football with the lads I never joined them socially, preferring to go straight home after a match.

This emotional isolation led me to do strange things, including trying out my singing voice in a most unusual way. High on the hills overlooking Oldham was a tuberculosis hospital. It was used by people who had contracted the deadly disease and were sent there to convalesce. In those days TB was a common illness, although today it has almost been eradicated. The hospital was a huge building, standing like a Gothic coliseum on the horizon, and I used to go up there and slip around the back. When I shouted at the enormous wall it would send a wonderful echo back, and this seemed to bring some comfort to my troubled being. I would stand there for hours, singing the hits of the day to myself and doing the actions too. If I was singing a Frank Sinatra song, then I would be Frank Sinatra; if I was singing an Elvis song, I was Elvis, swivelling hips and all. The echo would make me feel as if I was singing on a record or in a nightclub. If anybody had caught me I would have been carried away in a straitjacket, but I wouldn't have cared because I sounded great – or so I thought!

The boys in the football team always used to ask me to go with them to the dance halls in order to pick up some girls, but I always refused. The fear of rejection would kick in and I was scared that I would end up on my own. Despite being the 'place to be', the dance halls were a no-go area for me. Occasionally I ventured to the pub for a drink and somehow my mates must have known about my love of singing because they would always ask me to get up and perform. I always refused until I was drunk. When the beer started working, though, my confidence would build and I would belt out my favourite tune, 'They Tried To Tell Us We're Too Young'. If I was doing well I would stay there all night. The trouble was, I always thought I was doing well because by then I was drunk. The noise must have emptied a few pubs around Oldham.

The best time relaxing with the football team was at the end of the season when we celebrated by having a night out in Blackpool. Even if we'd had a bad season we never missed an opportunity for the yearly trip. This was before the advent of motorways and Blackpool was quite a long ride away across bumpy, winding roads. We would set off in a hired coach at about nine o'clock in the morning and stop for lunch, which was usually liquid. Then we would pile back onto our transport and resume our journey, stopping about 15 minutes later so that everyone could take a leak by the side of the road. This was an obligatory thing.

The journey normally took about three hours, but with all the stopping for roadside facilities along the way, it could take an hour longer. We would eventually arrive in Blackpool early in the afternoon. The pub-crawl began immediately and continued until it was time to go home, which was usually midnight. It was absolute chaos. Some guys would wander off and miss the coach back so we wouldn't see them for days; others would be throwing up all over the place and thinking they were having a great time. I'm sure that most of them couldn't remember what they were supposed to be celebrating, and I was no different. I would get drunk and throw up even though it always felt worse than dying. I think that's why today I don't drink heavily, or visit pubs much, as the thought of being drunk still repels me. Arriving home in the early hours of the morning, we would all have hangovers, but we would still congratulate each other on a fabulous day out. Sometimes it's better to be old!

After months of pestering by the football lads, I eventually agreed to go to a dance hall with them. The most popular one in Oldham was The Hill Stores. It was called this because the venue was over a furniture shop which had the same name. It was where all the young people would go, to dance and flirt with each other, and listen to The Jack Nelson Meteors, a dance band that played the hits of the day. I went there with the guys that night and was so nervous. I felt particularly conspicuous, as if I was wearing a bright orange suit or something luminous. Everyone seemed to be looking at me. On a football or cricket pitch I had no nerves at all, but away from the energy and excitement of the game I was extremely shy.

When I walked in, the band was playing and everybody was dancing. I instantly felt totally out of my depth – it was just the situation I dreaded. I made straight for the bar and downed a pint of beer quicker than a rabbit can get down a hole. This was followed by another. Soon my confidence started to grow and I began to relax. Some of the boys started to drift off looking for girls to dance with and I was left with just a couple of mates. We continued to make small talk, but then I noticed a girl across the dance hall who made my heart jump. She was surrounded by boys and was obviously very popular.

She reminded me of the crush I had on a big pop star of the time, Doris Day. Although the girl I was eyeing had only the blonde hair and not the body beautiful of my idol, she still looked good enough to me. In fact, the more I looked at her, the more gorgeous she became. I thought about going over, but once again my old friend rejection sat on my shoulder. Another beer, however, and I felt confidence starting to run through me. With my greased, slicked-back hair and my drainpipe trousers I thought I looked pretty good. I might stand a chance. It was now or never.

Taking a deep breath, I made my way over to where this girl was sitting and asked her in my best controlled voice to dance. To my amazement she immediately agreed! I must have danced all right, because we stayed together for the whole evening. Her name was Margaret, and her father was a butcher who owned his own shop in Oldham. In my insecure mind she seemed a whole league above me. After all, she came from a middle-class family and I was working class. By the end of the night, however, my feelings of inadequacy had evaporated. We danced and talked, and I must have been doing OK because she said she would go out with me. From this chance meeting started a long courtship.

Margaret and I continued to see each other for a few weeks, and then the day came when I had to meet her parents. Margaret told me that Frank and Laura had invited me to tea, and she was both excited and nervous about it. She can't have been as nervous as me. When the day came I put on my best suit and headed for their shop. I stood on the doorstep with my heart in my mouth, wondering whether I had done the right thing or not. Margaret must have understood my fear, because when I rang the doorbell she opened the door, gave me a huge smile, took my hand and guided me into the front room.

Her parents stood up to greet me and invited me to sit down with them. I felt like a pauper in a palace. Even though they were only butchers and lived above the shop, to me they seemed to have everything. I certainly felt out of my depth when we sat at the dinner table and Margaret's mother brought out a salad. Lying on top was a special fork and spoon set. I had never seen anything like them in my life. In fact, we never ate salad at home – that was reserved for rich people. Margaret's mother offered me the salad bowl and the utensils sat staring me right in the face for some while, because I didn't know how to use them. Rather than embarrass myself, I declined on the pretext that I would have some later. If I could wait until someone else had some, I would be able to discover how to get the salad from the bowl to my plate.

I eventually got through the meal without making too much of a fool of myself and I must have passed the test because they invited me back the following week. I became part of the family, often joining them for meals to practise my table skills, and after only a few months Margaret's parents must have suspected that marriage was on the menu.

We had some great times when we were courting, but also some disasters. Margaret and I and a couple of friends decided to have a weekend away one summer. Margate seemed to be at the other side of the world from Oldham, so this was adventure on a grand scale for us. We made arrangements to borrow her dad's car and set off. After six hours of driving we arrived and booked ourselves into a bed and breakfast. We were told that one of the rules was that we had to be out of the guesthouse after breakfast and we weren't allowed back until the time of the evening meal, even though we weren't eating there. This didn't bother us. We reckoned we would spend the day in the sun on the beach and the evening in a pub. We were covered, so we thought.

Pretending to be Mr and Mrs Derbyshire, we went up to our bedroom for a night of fun and games and it was late when we finally fell asleep. When the next morning came, it was bucketing down outside. I'm not sure if even Noah's Ark could have withstood the downpour. We had our breakfast and kept looking at the landlady pleadingly, but it was all to no avail. After breakfast she made us leave until the evening. We put our raincoats on and started to walk down to the seafront. After about three hours we had used up all our money in the slot machines. We spent the rest of our adventure in Margate sitting in the car playing cards, with the rain never ceasing. Even now, when Bobby and I go back to Margate to do a gig, the memory of that weekend comes flooding back to me – and the strange thing is, it's always raining.

After a few years of courting, Margaret and I got married in 1959 and spent our honeymoon in London. We planned to wait a few years before we had any children so that we could get on our feet financially, but Margaret fell pregnant straightaway and we had our first child exactly nine months from the date of our honeymoon. Even so, we were extremely excited about having a baby in the family.

On the day of the birth I went to work as usual. During the day Margaret was rushed into hospital in labour. In those days there were no mobile phones, so someone from the hospital contacted my foreman with the news that I was the proud father of a baby boy. When he told me, I went crazy. I was absolutely ecstatic. I had always wanted a son and I had been successful on

my first try! I ran around the building site telling everybody about my new son. All day I dreamed about him
doing the things I hadn't done. Football, cricket, college
– I had everything planned for him, and he was only a
few hours old.

After work I dashed home to get changed so that I
could go to the hospital to visit Margaret and my new
son. When I got home Margaret's father was waiting for
me. 'Sit down, Tom,' he said. 'I have some news from
the hospital.'

Dread began to rush through my mind. Was Margaret
all right? Was my son all right? 'What is it?' I asked,
trying to prepare myself for the bad news.

'Well, the doctors are furious,' he began. 'A young
nurse saw the baby and mistook the umbilical cord
for a willy. So, Tom lad, you're the father of a baby girl,
not a boy!'

I was stunned. In one second my longed-for son had
turned into a girl. To say I was disappointed is an under-
statement. I got changed and headed gloomily for the
hospital. I knew I would have to hide my feelings from
Margaret. The minute I saw my daughter, however, my
sadness vanished. She was the most gorgeous baby I had
ever seen. All thoughts of a son disappeared from my
head. I was now the father of the most beautiful little girl
in the world. We named her Janette and I told Margaret
that I was so proud of her and my daughter. Before long
we were all at home together, just like a storybook family.

We bought our first terraced house in Chelsfield,
considered quite a posh part of Oldham, for £1,200, and
were extremely pleased with what we had achieved.
Two years later another baby girl arrived, and we named
her Julie. She was just as beautiful as our first daughter.

ROCK ON, TOMMY!

Our family was complete, and we set about building a life together. I continued to move from job to job, but Margaret opened a hairdresser's shop at the front of the house. Life was idyllic – until I started work at an engineering firm, and there my life was to change for ever. I was to lose a family but gain a lifelong friend.

CHAPTER THREE

THE BLACK AND TANS

As Bobby and Tommy recall their early years, the parallels that unfold are quite astonishing. Whilst Tommy was courting, Bobby was not far behind, and was making sure he was getting the most out of life. Having been caught up in the madness of the rock'n'roll days, his 1950s world was a whirlwind of records and fashion. The future seemed an eternity away; all that mattered was the 'now'.

I was having a fantastic time. For me there was no future, just the minute I was living in. At 14 I had a girlfriend and thought that everybody over 20 was old. (My girlfriend suffered awfully from acne, but it wasn't so bad because on boring nights I used to draw dot to dot on her face.)

My libido had kicked in with an explosion early on, and I soon noticed that girls had other things besides long hair and dolls. A combination of hormones and inquisitiveness caused me to pop into a newsagent's one day, and when the owner of the shop wasn't looking I stole a magazine called *Parade*, shoving it under my coat.

Parade was looked upon then as a racy men's magazine, with pictures of girls in provocative poses.

The funny thing is, you could hardly see anything, but it was enough to get my head spinning. Today the *Sun* newspaper is more shocking. *Parade* first caught my eye at the local newsagent's where I was employed as a paperboy. There weren't too many of these magazines knocking around then and I think the most famous was *Tit Bits*. This magazine showed girls in skimpy bikinis, but never topless, and included some sexy stories. *Parade* was the raunchier one because it would occasionally show topless models. The first time I saw it, I was delivering my papers when I pulled out something with a glossy cover which I glanced through. It blew my mind – I had never seen anything so exciting in my life. I forgot all about my paper round and just leaned against the wall and read it with eyes and everything else boggling. The papers were very late that morning, but after that I was determined to get my own copy by hook or by crook.

Now, running home with my 'catch' under my armpit, I kept looking over my shoulder expecting to see the shop owner hot on my heels. He wasn't, of course, and he obviously hadn't noticed. As I ran, my feelings ran with me, hovering somewhere between victory and guilt. I reached home and, with my heart beating wildly, ran quickly up-stairs to my bedroom. There was an air vent high up on the wall and it had a little flap that could be opened and shut. I stood on the edge of the bed and put my stolen magazine inside the vent, closing the flap behind it.

I would take the magazine out of its secret hiding place at every chance and ogle over the pictures of gorgeous girls showing as much as they dared. After about two days, by which time I had nearly read the pictures right off the page, I was sitting watching television when my mother calmly said to my dad, 'Bob, that vent needs cleaning in our Robert's room.'

My heart leapt into my mouth. She looked at me and I knew that she had discovered my secret. I made some feeble excuse and dashed upstairs, wondering whether she had taken it. I began to shake, feeling as though I had committed something awful like a murder. I opened the flap of the air vent and there sat my *Parade*. She hadn't found it after all. I quickly ripped it up and then wondered what I could do to destroy it. The only way to get rid of it quickly, I realized, was to flush it down the toilet.

Crossing the landing with my beloved *Parade* pushed up my jumper was a horrendous moment. Fully expecting my mother or father to catch me red-handed, I eventually made it to the bathroom with a sigh of relief and locked the door behind me. I frantically started to tear the magazine up into smaller pieces, but then it suddenly occurred to me that the ripping sound was probably being heard by the whole street. I panicked, thinking they could also hear me downstairs. I stopped mid-tear and wondered what I was going to do with this half-destroyed magazine. My eyes alighted on the taps. 'That's it!' I thought. Running water would cover the sound of the paper tearing. What a genius!

With the water gushing out, I finished off the job and eventually turned the magazine into tiny slivers of paper, managing to flush the whole lot down the loo, bundle after bundle. I watched as the last piece of the magazine went round and round in the bottom of the bowl before being sucked down. It seemed to take for ever, and with all the flushing and water sounds, those nearby must have thought I had a serious bowel problem. Eventually the last piece of evidence disappeared, and I never brought a magazine home again. The pressure of being discovered was too much. Every time I went to the bathroom after that, I worried that the paper strips might have blocked the pan, and the evidence would suddenly be washed up to haunt me.

I was very relieved that I hadn't been found out by my mother, but many years later I learned that she had in fact found the magazine, but had left it where it was to save me from embarrassment. She understood about children growing up and letting things take their natural course, and helped me quietly along the way.

When I left school I went straight into the cotton mill where my mother and sisters worked, so it seemed like a natural progression. My first job was in the 'Devil Hole'. It was called this because it was one of the dirtiest jobs, at the start of the chain where the bales of cotton arrived. They would be ripped open by us and fed into machines that tore the cotton apart and fed it onto rolls. These would be taken up to the spinners, who would spin the cotton onto the bobbins. I was treated a little better than most because my mother and sisters were well liked and had been there some years before me. Even in a cotton mill there's a class system. The lowest job was in the 'Devil Hole', with the spinners being quite high up in the respect chain.

As the cotton mill wasn't far from our house I would go home with my mother and sisters for lunch. Shaw was known as a 'cotton village'. There were more mills in Shaw than in any other place in Lancashire. It was an accepted thing that you went to work in the mill, and I followed suit. At that time I didn't have any ambitions to do anything else. I was like any other 15-year-old, just happy enjoying my social life. The future seemed a long way away, but after about six months I started to hate every minute of working in the mill. During the summer when the sun was shining I would set off to work at seven in the morning and would then have to go into this dark and dismal place, leaving the beauty of the day behind. The more this happened, the more I thought about what I was missing, and the more I felt I needed to get away from the mill and its depressiveness.

Trying to avoid offers of work which would incarcerate me inside for the whole day, I soon managed to get a job working outside with a firm of builders. Joining Pogson and Sons proved to be one of the best things I did as a youth. Leaving the dark surroundings of the cotton mill, I was thrust immediately into a job that meant working outside most of the time. It gave me a sense of freedom which helped me feel wonderfully alive. When I say it was a firm of builders, it actually just consisted of father and son. They were both named John, so I called the father 'Big John' and the son just 'John'. They did a variety of jobs, including odd repairs in people's homes, working in schools, plastering, that sort of thing. The two Johns made me very welcome and I soon settled in, but not before I had the shock of my life.

I had been with them for just two days when Big John said that we had a job to do in the local mortuary. He explained that the walls needed painting with a certain substance and we had the responsibility of this 'unique' job. I had never been in a mortuary before, let alone seen a dead body. Come to think of it, I had never even seen anybody really ill. As we loaded the wagon with the necessary materials and set off for the mortuary, I was feeling very apprehensive, wondering what I was going to find there. It was only a small mortuary that fitted two bodies, so I was hoping in my heart that nobody had died that morning. I was told that with the ladders and tools it would be a tight squeeze getting past the corpses easily, and I wasn't looking forward to that at all.

We started to unload the wagon, and then Big John said that he had forgotten some tools and that I would have to go back to get them. I dutifully set off for the builder's yard and, finding the tools, returned to the mortuary. As I approached the building all sorts of things started to race through my mind. Would a body be there? What would it look like? Would I have to touch it? My mind was a blur of questions. When I reached the door I heard Big John singing inside. Relief spread through my body. If he was singing, then in all probability there would be no corpses in there. I took a deep breath and walked through the door. What I saw made me freeze.

On the slab was a lifeless body with a cover on it, but on the floor to one side was a pile of bloody meat that looked like someone had recently been disembowelled. I dropped the tools with a yell and ran off as fast as my legs could carry me. I ran all the way home, vowing never to go back again. I burst into the house and blurted out my terrible discovery to my mother. She told me not to be silly as that sort of thing didn't happen – but she hadn't seen what I had seen.

About half an hour later Big John and his son came walking down the garden path and I noticed his son was laughing. They came into the house and proceeded to tell me that they had played a trick on me and that they were sorry. The 'intestines' were some pieces of old meat that they had borrowed from the butcher. They had put the meat on the floor just to see my reaction. They certainly hadn't expected me to behave in the way I did. They apologized once more and asked me to come back to work. By this time I had calmed down and started to laugh about it myself. I went back to work with them at the mortuary. They hadn't kidded me about the body, which was still there, but for some reason it didn't frighten me any more and I simply worked around it. I will never forget the day that I was terrified by a piece of old meat from the butcher's, though.

Having a vivid imagination has been my downfall more than once. It doesn't help when you work with a couple of practical jokers. One day we had a job to do on a church. Big John had decided to send his son and myself on the job alone, as he was taking the weekend off. We were told that the steeple was leaning and needed straightening. To get into the belfry we had to climb a dark spiral staircase that led straight up with tiny openings in the wall every so often to allow in the minimum of light. Young John and I climbed the stone steps high into the belfry and set about deciding how we were going to straighten the steeple. It was really spooky up there. The only light coming in was from the little windows on the spiral staircase, and with the wind whistling around the eaves it created a very scary atmosphere.

Young John told me that the belfry was haunted and that an old man with a hunched back had hung himself from the bells many years ago. I told him not to be stupid, but he insisted and started to convince me. He said that if I watched the staircase I would see spirits going up and down. I looked at the stairs, and it was true. I could see shadows rising and falling. I dismissed it from my mind and told him we had better get on with our work. I didn't want to work, but anything was better than his ghost stories.

Halfway through the morning John said that he was going to get some sandwiches for our lunch and left me alone. The wind started to howl and it circulated inside the huge bells to make a ghostly moaning sound. The whole place became very eerie as my imagination took over. I stopped what I was doing and stared at the shadows moving up and down the stairs. Suddenly a moaning sound came from the bottom of the staircase. I shouted for John, but there was no answer. A shadow different from all the rest appeared and started to move up the stairs. 'John!' I shouted again, but still there was no answer. The large shadow had now started to take on a clearer shape, and it looked like an old man with a hunched back to me. The air became even blacker and the stirring of the bells seemed almost deafening. 'John, is that you?' I almost screamed. The hunchbacked shadow came further up the stairs and panic attacked me. My imagination was now running at full speed.

Panic-stricken, I picked up an iron bar and hid just round the corner at the top of the stairs. I waited with baited breath and as the figure entered the room my reflexes took over and I swung at it with the iron bar. The figure dropped what it was carrying and shouted 'Bobby!' It was John. Luckily I hadn't hurt him, but he looked pretty shocked.

As I watched him he broke into a laugh and explained what I had seen. He was the man's figure, and the sack he had been carrying over his shoulder completed the form of the hunchback. The other shadows were made by cars going up and down the street way below us. Every time a car went along the street it made a moving shadow on the spiral staircase. I felt so stupid. John laughed and laughed. He never let me forget it. Even when I see him today he still talks about it.

I think John took some pleasure in shocking me. A few months later he announced he had something to show me. He led me into a tumbledown wooden building at the back of the timber yard that I'm sure a gentle wind could have blown over. I followed him upstairs, hoping the steps wouldn't give way. When he opened the door I stared in amazement. There were about 200 young chicks chirping and running about as if they were having a day out at Disney World. It was an unbelievable sight.

'What are you going to do with these then, John?' I asked.

'Oh,' he replied, smiling, 'I'm going to feed them up for Christmas and then sell them.'

It was as if he had suddenly become the new Bernard Matthews. I just accepted what he said with a shake of my head and went back to work. The months passed and I noticed his frequent daily journeys to the dilapidated building as he diligently fed his chicks. About a week before Christmas he stood before me with a huge grin on his face.

'Come on, Bob, it's chicken day!'

'What do you mean?' I asked. 'Aren't we supposed to be working?'

'Not today, my dad has given us the day off,' came the reply.

'What about my money?' I said, thinking I was about to lose a day's pay.

'Don't worry, I'm paying you, so you'll be working with me today. So come on – as I said, it's chicken day!' and he started off towards his tumbledown shack. When we went upstairs I got the shock of my life once more. The 200 chicks had turned into huge hens. They seemed monstrous, and the noise they made was deafening. They were strutting and clucking as if they didn't have a care in the world. They were everywhere. Some were perched in the rafters, some on tables, some sat on benches, others strutted around the floor. Some of them looked at me and I stared back, lost for words.

Then I said, 'When you said, "It's chicken day," what did you mean?'

John looked at me with his eyes popping out like an actor from one of the silent horror movies. 'We're going to kill and pluck them,' he replied.

It was my turn to look like something out of a horror movie. 'I can't do that!' I answered. 'I've never killed anything in my life!'

He stared at me as if I was from a different planet. 'Don't be a tart, Bobby! We're only killing some hens, so that people can have Christmas dinner.'

His logic didn't seem to make sense to me. He was acting as if he was the chickens' benefactor instead of making a few bob out of them all. He had left me with no choice, however, because I didn't want to appear a wimp or look as if I wasn't capable of killing hens. 'Well,' I said, 'I've killed things before like frogs and so on, but I've never killed a hen.' I realized how wimpy that sounded, but John didn't seem to notice.

'Right, let's get started then.' He grabbed the nearest hen and handed it straight to me. I hated the feel of it in my arms – it felt sort of squashy! One wing got loose and it started to flap. It was a horrible feeling and inside I was starting to panic, but somehow I managed to control it. As the bird flapped and squawked for all it was worth, John said, 'Put it against this table, so that its head is just underneath.' I would have done anything at that moment to stop it flapping. Obediently I held the hen with its head just under the table edge. The hen instinctively lifted its head onto the top so that its neck was lying flat on the table ... and WHACK! John hit it with a piece of wood right across its neck.

I jumped back in shock and dropped the hen, which fell to the floor stone dead, although it kept twitching as if it was alive. It wasn't, it was just the nerves settling down, but it seemed horrible to me. I felt as if I had committed a murder. We both stood there looking down at the hen, and I started to feel sick. Looking at our handiwork, John said, 'Brilliant, let's do the rest.'

'Oh man,' I thought to myself. 'What have I let myself in for?'

The rest of the afternoon was spent chasing hens and killing them. After about 50 of them I got over my squeamishness and before long I was handling the hens like an old-time chicken farmer. We eventually killed them all and John offered to pay me overtime if I would stay and help him to pluck them. I agreed and at about 10 o'clock that night I left the building looking as if I had been tarred and feathered. Thankfully, that was my first and last forage into the slaughter of hens and it was many months before I could eat chicken again. John did go on to sell his chickens to the local butchers, and after Christmas, when people told me they had eaten a chicken dinner, I always wondered if it had been one of ours.

My days with Pogson's were happy times. Big John

took me under his wing and treated me just like a son. He died many years ago, but every now and again he comes into my mind and I think about the good times. I miss him.

By now I had started back in show business too. The teddy boy era had ended and I found the desire to sing again. I started a proper act with my girlfriend Joan, our Mavis and my friend Trevor. We called ourselves The Black and Tans because Joan, Mavis and Trevor all had red hair and I had black hair. We thought it was a good name until we did a few Irish clubs, and then we realized that it wasn't that good, as the Black and Tans were an old British regiment which had fought the Irish. That caused a few comments!

I never got tired working during the day and singing at night, because I classed singing with The Black and Tans as my leisure time and it didn't seem like work at all. We did the clubs at weekends and worked normally during the week. We even entered the Pontins talent competition on holiday and got through to the final. We were beaten by a group who sounded really great. Even though they were good, however, I didn't think they were as good as us. I remember that when the competition had finished and we were waiting for the judges to vote, I knew in my heart that we had won, because we had gone down the best with the audience. When the judges announced that this other group had won, the audience went crazy. They started to stamp their feet and bang the tables. They weren't pleased and had obviously wanted us to win. The judges' decision was final, of course, but for the rest of our time at the camp people kept coming up to us and saying, 'You were robbed!'

THE BLACK AND TANS

We all became very close and never went anywhere without each other. Then Mavis started courting Trevor and our foursome was complete. We did everything together. If one of us went to the cinema, you could guarantee that the other three would follow.

As a teenager my only problem was that I liked violence. I loved the thrill it gave me, even though I wasn't that good at it. In fact I was the only kid in Oldham with a cauliflower bottom! I certainly didn't attack my dad because I had enormous respect for him, and found it abhorrent whenever my friends turned on their parents, but anyone else was fair game. I think I just loved violence for the sake of it. It gave me a rush of excitement that I found exhilarating. It didn't make me feel 'more like a man' or anything like that – it was just something that gave me an extra kick. Through violence I achieved a sense of power and excitement, wondering whether I could beat the other bloke or not.

Sitting in a dance hall or just walking down the street, I would try and stare somebody out. I loved to watch them become more and more intimidated and would continue to glare at them until they either said something or turned away. I only stared at other guys to start a fight, and considering that I was only five foot two and weighed eight and a half stone, it's a wonder that I wasn't punch-drunk. I always came away the victor, though – except for once.

Our gang – Joan, Mavis, Trevor and I – were strolling down Yorkshire Street in Oldham when we saw two guys walking towards us. When they reached us they tried to walk around us, but I wasn't having that, oh no. I bumped into one of them. He was a big guy and his mate was just a little bigger than I was. Their size didn't bother me, however, because I had Trevor with me and he was big too.

'Have you got a problem?' I asked, knowing that this was a real confrontation.

'Yes,' the big guy replied. 'You!'

'Well, what are you going to do about it?' I said, trying to make myself taller than I was.

'There's two of you and two of us,' he said. 'Let's sort it out.'

I looked at Trevor and he nodded; he was always a man of few words. There was a back alley just opposite the place where we were standing, so I said to them, 'OK, let's get it on.'

I started to walk towards the alley and Mavis and Joan started shouting at us not to be so stupid, but the adrenaline was already flowing. As soon as we got into the alley I turned, but I was too late. One of the guys hit me square on the mouth. I never saw it coming, and now blood was gushing out from my numb and swollen lips. I was filled with an outraged passion to get him back, and from then on it was a free-for-all. Trevor was handling the other guy all right, but I was being beaten like a punchbag – and I was meant to be the tough one! I got the biggest beating of my life that day. Suddenly the girls came running into the alley shouting that the police were coming. The two guys jumped up and ran away, leaving me lying on the floor, bleeding like a stuck pig. Trevor didn't have a mark on him.

The others helped me up and we started walking out of the alley, pretending nothing had happened. When we reached Yorkshire Street two policemen ran past us into the alley. They hadn't even noticed me bleeding, and when they had disappeared we started to run.

I made all the excuses in the world for my abysmal macho performance. I wasn't ready! It was too dark! He took me by surprise! The truth of the matter was that the guy had beaten me squarely. Being beaten only enhanced my desire for more violence, although I was no different from hundreds of other young teenage boys growing up in the north of England.

It seemed that my life on the street was in total contrast to my life on the stage. I was a little devil one minute and a little angel with The Black and Tans the next. The act worked well, but for several reasons it suddenly stopped. Trevor and Mavis were getting married, Joan didn't want to do it any more without them, and so it just came to a natural end.

I was very sad at the parting, but we all continued to be close friends and I decided to sing on my own. It gave me such a buzz that it was difficult to let go. To be in show biz you have to be a show-off, and this was exactly what I was. I loved the applause. Of course, I had been singing for some time now and it had become second nature to me. The extra pocket money didn't have to be shared between three others any longer either. It felt very strange being on stage alone, but I started to relish it. With my zest for life and outgoing personality I was a 'natural'. It was the only time that I was truly happy. I didn't care what I did, as long as I got a chance to entertain people. The only thing I thought I would never be was a comedian.

Joan and I had started to save up to get married and suddenly we got into the 'getting married' routine of staying in at nights so that we could save money for the wedding. During this time 'proper' work wasn't very good. The winter was bad so there was no building work. I applied for many posts and eventually ended up as a labourer at an engineering firm in Oldham.

Soon after that, Joan and I tied the knot. We bought a small terraced house and I felt as if I owned the world. Before long Joan fell pregnant and our first child, Robert, was born. Joan had always been frightened of hospitals, so she decided to have the baby at home. It was a nightmare. I was only young and didn't have a clue what to do. As the day of the birth came closer Joan's mother took over. The midwife was coming every day and things started to get a bit hectic. When Joan went into labour I ran around the corner to her mother's house for help. The midwife arrived and I was made to wait downstairs until it was all over. I just sat there wondering what was going on, and when I heard the baby cry for the first time my heart stood still.

Minutes later Joan's mother shouted down to me that it was OK to go up and see our new baby. I dashed upstairs and there he was, lying in the crib. I looked at him and was horrified because he had bloody marks on his face. I turned on the midwife and shouted at her, 'What are all those marks on my child's face?'

She started to laugh and so did Joan's mother. 'It's all right, Mr Harper,' she said through her laughter. 'I haven't washed him yet.'

I didn't understand what she meant until she explained that they weren't marks at all, just stains from being born. She told me to get Joan something to eat and when I got back she would have washed the child. I ran to the shop and bought Joan some jam cake. When I got back our Robert was transformed into a beautiful child with not a mark on him. I gave the jam cake to

Joan and she just smiled. Joan's mother took the cake off her and proceeded to give me a dressing down. Joan needed something more substantial than jam cake, she told me in no uncertain terms. I had thought that the sugar would give her some energy. Well, I didn't pretend to be the Brain of Britain!

After a couple of years our second child arrived. It was another boy and we named him Darren. Everything should have been perfect now, but with the struggle to repay our mortgage alongside our youthful ignorance of the burden of hire purchase we found ourselves struggling under a mountain of debt. Inevitably our home was repossessed by the bank and we ended up in a council house on one of the roughest estates in Oldham. It was a bad time for all of us, but I was determined that we would survive. I still had something up my sleeve.

A few years earlier I had approached the foreman at the engineering firm, a man called Jack Booth, and asked him if I could be a welder. In those days welding was considered a trade. I liked the way that welders got a lot of respect from the other workers in the factory. Respect was obviously something I was searching for. I looked for it in the fights I caused; I looked for it in the audiences' applause; now I was looking for it at work. I also reckoned that if I was going to do something with my life, I might as well be a welder.

I would have to go to college one day a week, and even at 18 years of age I still needed Jack's permission for this. 'Look, lad,' he said. 'You're too old to go to college now, so just accept it. You're a labourer, and that's what you always will be.'

'No I won't,' I replied, feeling the anger grow inside me. 'Someday I'll be a welder.'

Jack just smirked at me and said, 'Just get back to your job or I'll dock your wages.' I went back to my labouring feeling very sad because he had taken the wind out of my sails, but he had also made me more determined to prove him wrong. I enrolled at the college anyway, and started to go to night school in my free time, three times a week. If I could get my City and Guilds certificate it would prove that I was a tradesman and not just another worker.

During the day I was labouring and at night I was going to college and studying, as well as singing in the clubs at weekends. After three years of hard slog I got my City and Guilds certificate. I was now a tradesman. The day after I gained my new credibility I went into work and waited until the foreman walked past.

'Can I have a word with you, Jack?' I asked him.

'What is it, Harper?' he answered, clearly indicating that he didn't have time to talk to me.

'I asked you three years ago if I could be a welder,' I said.

'Yes, I remember,' he replied, as if our conversation was irrelevant.

'Well,' I continued, 'I still want to be one.'

He looked at me as if I had lost my mind. 'Are you crackers, Harper?' he said. 'You have to start as an apprentice to be a welder and you're just a labourer.'

I stood up to my full height and puffed my chest out. This was the moment I had been waiting for these last three years. 'I'm not a labourer any more, Jack,' I said.

'What do you mean?' he answered, now obviously interested in what I had to say.

I pulled my City and Guilds certificate out of my pocket and proudly showed it to him. 'I'm a welder now.'

He looked at my certificate with a puzzled expression on his face. 'Where did you get this?' he asked.

I told him how I had been going to night school for three years and how I had studied in my own time. 'Well, lad,' he said eventually, 'well done. So answer me this: what are you doing here? Shouldn't you be in the welding bay with the other welders if you're a welder?'

'Well, yes, I suppose so,' I answered, a little dumbfounded at his response.

'Go on then, lad,' he said. 'Get welding.'

'Thanks Jack,' I replied and set off to join the other welders.

'Harper!' Jack shouted back to me. 'I'll put you on tradesman's wages from today!'

It was a great thrill for me to have proved the foreman wrong. With my family, my singing and now my promotion as a welder, I didn't think life could get much better. How was I to know that I would soon be teaming up with someone who was to change my life for ever?

CHAPTER FOUR

ROCK 'N' ROLL

Tommy's secret desire to become a singer continued to fill his thoughts day and night, but it was an ambition that he kept well hidden from his mates. Singing in the pub at night was one thing; actually going into show business was quite another. He knew he would be well ribbed at work if he ever declared such an interest. No, he was a worker and a worker he would stay. Or so he thought.

Standing nervously like a little boy on his first day at school, I wondered how long this latest job would last. The day I started work at the engineering firm Boden Trailers was just as bad as all the other first days. I had got the work through a guy named Dennis Phipps, who happened to be my cousin's husband. I had worked outside for most of my adult life, so to be working inside was a new challenge for me. At least it would be a lot warmer, I thought. I went into the factory and stood by the door waiting to be assigned to a job. I didn't know anyone and there were about 500 other guys there, but no one spoke to me as I stood alone.

Suddenly this bloke rushed in through the door like a cyclone, looked at me and said, 'Hello cock, how are you?' (I feel I must clear things up a little at this point. The word 'cock' is a slang word that is native to Oldham, really. It means 'friend'.) The thing that immediately struck me about this guy was his height. He was really small with a mop of black hair that stood up as if he had just put his finger in a socket. The best way of describing my first sight of him would be to say that if he were a dog he would have been a Jack Russell. After he had greeted me in his own inimitable way, he dashed past me and that was the last I saw of him. I didn't even know his name.

The foreman eventually arrived and I was put in the fitter welder section. As part of a team of three, I would create the initial framework for the vehicles we were producing before passing it on to the next section. Ironically, the funny little man I had seen earlier worked in the next section.

I settled down to what I hoped would be a secure job at last. Eventually I got to know some of the guys. I was surprised to find that adapting to inside work wasn't that difficult and started to enjoy the camaraderie that comes when people work together.

In Oldham, like the rest of the country, Friday night was deemed 'lads' night out'. Some of the guys from Bodens would have a night on the town and I was no exception. I started having my Friday night drink with a guy called Albert Bates and we would go around Oldham from pub to pub. More often than not, we would bump into the funny guy with the electric hair who had said 'hello' on my first day. I soon discovered that his name was Bobby.

I saw Bobby at Bodens, but I really got to know him when I kept bumping into him on our nights out. He was very thin and looked as if he only weighed about eight stone. He looked to me like one of those little rascals who would always be in trouble. I bet my mates that he'd been the kind of kid who was always being belted by his mother for being cheeky. I also mulled over the fact that his size would obviously mean that he needed someone to sort his fights out for him. I was unaware then that he was often the cause of the fights in the first place!

I had a strange fascination with this guy, though I couldn't work out exactly what it was that made us click. Bobby was smaller and younger than me and I found myself feeling protective of him, like an older brother might feel towards a younger one. As I got to know Bobby better I realized that he had very few in-between moods. He was either flying high as a kite or feeling really down. I suppose I'm lucky in a way because I'm pretty stable emotionally, and I didn't really understand these peaks and troughs.

Bobby and I soon became close friends, and I hoped that we could play football together. It was just my luck that my lifelong partner-to-be wasn't interested in sport at all. He wouldn't know one end of a cricket bat from the other, and as for football, forget it, it might have been invented by aliens as far as he's concerned. However, I soon found out that there were other, deeper interests that we shared.

Bobby and I started to go out together at nights on a regular basis. I even went to see him sing in the local clubs at weekends. The first time I saw Bobby perform was at a little working men's club just outside Oldham. When he got up to sing at the Royton British Legion Club I was surprised at how good he was. He had never really struck me as a singer because all the stars of the day were tall with quiffed hair, quite the opposite to Bobby. His choice of material was pretty predictable, but he sang one song that I thought was really strange because it was so old. It was out of place with all his other numbers and didn't suit him at all. It was called 'My Mother's Eyes'. Although it was obviously of sentimental value, he never explained why he sang it, but I can say after all these years: Bobby, it was rubbish! I suppose it just goes to show that you can't always croon the tunes that mean the most to you; you have to please the public first.

Despite continually hearing this awful song I persevered, watching Bobby sing in several different venues. I was never jealous that it was Bobby up there and not me, but it did help to plant my own seeds of determination deeper. Soon Bobby took a weekend residency as a drummer at the Middleton Working Men's Club and another ritual began. Every Friday the guys and I would go down to the club and have a drink with Bobby between his sets on stage. At about 10 o'clock we would leave to go to the Candlelight Club, where Bobby would join us later and we could drink until two in the morning.

One night as we were drinking and talking, Bobby said to me, 'Why don't you get a kit of drums? I'll teach you to drum.'

'OK,' I replied, not realizing that this was the moment when my life was going to change gear for ever. The next day I approached my father-in-law and borrowed £200 to buy a drum kit, went down to the local music shop and purchased my prize. When I eagerly told Bobby, he was so surprised that it made me wonder if he had been drunk when he had originally put forward the idea. My heart sank for a moment as I contemplated the possibility of having been set up by my new friend. Rejection lurked once more, until a moment later his eyes lit up and he arranged to come over to my house the next day to begin lessons.

I practised what he taught me over the next few evenings as if it could save my life. Even though I tried to drum when the family were out, I don't know what the neighbours thought! I quickly picked up the technique and before long I was pretty proficient. In a short space of time, in fact, I became a better drummer than Bobby.

The turnover of acts in clubs is pretty fast. Once they've seen you, you can't really go back there for some time. This fitted Bobby's plan of activities, as I noticed that he quickly got bored doing the same thing every night in the same place. It wasn't long before he stopped drumming at the club and suggested that we start a trio with the pianist who was also resident there. Stan Moores also worked at the factory with us. I readily agreed. Was this the time for me to put all my years of singing practice behind the hospital wall into real action?

My first step on the show-business ladder was not to be up front, however. I was the drummer – it was Bobby who crooned over the front row. We called ourselves The Stan Moores Trio and got booked for a few gigs which seemed to go down very well, and we obviously enjoyed working together. Our work at the factory continued as usual, but Stan was involved in more than just his day job. He still worked solo weekends at the club and ran a shop on the side. With Stan being unavailable more times than not, the trio quickly faded.

It was too late for me, though – the show business bug had bitten me deep. When Bobby suggested that we start a singing act together with a friend of ours, Ronnie Ravey, I jumped at the chance. That idea didn't work because Ronnie didn't seem to turn up for practices either. I commented to Bobby that our rehearsals were becoming more like a double act than a trio and, as if ordained, we ended up with just the two of us. Bobby was always full of ideas. His eyes would twinkle at me while a new idea formed in his head. This began to set the basis for our working relationship together, as Bobby looked after the artistic side and I managed the business areas, probably because it has always been easier for me to say a firm 'no'.

We started serious rehearsals at my house three evenings a week, during which Bobby tried to come up with a plan to make us different from all the other singers around. On one rehearsal day I could see Bobby getting more and more frustrated with me. He kept looking over to where I was standing and frowning. Eventually he asked if I had a full-length mirror in the house. When I heaved it into the room he proceeded to prop it up against the wall, turned to me and told me to sing watching myself in the mirror. It felt a bit self-indulgent and I reacted strongly against the suggestion, which I protested would make me look like a 'pansy'. Only girlies and posers watched themselves in a mirror, and I told Bobby in no uncertain terms to 'naff off'. I wasn't going to act like a pervert and I didn't believe I was that vain.

Bobby kept going on at me. When I sang I was too stiff, he said, and I needed to relax more. 'If you're not enjoying it, then the audience won't either,' he explained.

'Who do you want me to be, Elvis Presley?' I argued.

'You'll never be that good!' he replied.

Eventually I gave in and tried it (after all, I'd been doing much the same thing in my private singing sessions behind the hospital). So there I was, standing in front of the mirror singing to myself, with Bobby urging me to move my legs in time to the music. If any of the guys we worked with had seen these two butch labourers singing and dancing in front of a mirror, they would have thought we had finally come out of the closet as the first two gay welders in Oldham. Amazingly, though, it worked and I felt free and easy and comfortable with the way I looked. I suddenly realized this was a great lesson for me and I began to trust Bobby's suggestions, admiring the natural feel he had for the business. He seemed to know by intuition what would work. It wasn't long before we were ready to start our real assault on the world of show business.

Our nights of rehearsal built up our confidence to the point where we believed we were the best and that audiences would be knocked off their feet when they saw us. Visions of having our names in lights and on the door of the star dressing room, along with agents and managers negotiating requests from television producers, filled our waking as well as our sleeping hours. How wrong we were! We should have known simply from the name we eventually picked that immediate, world-beating success would not be ours. We called ourselves – wait for it – Bobby and Stevie Rhythm. It was so corny that I still shudder to repeat it and, looking back, it sounds more like a method of family planning than a singing act. Somehow it didn't matter. I was beginning to realize my secret ambition at last.

Bobby was quickly proving his love and understanding of performance, and teaching Tommy fired his passion even more. The inner drive to make what he did on stage work became an increasing obsession. Somehow, he felt, there was a missing element to the act that he hadn't noticed. He was determined to find it, and nothing was going to stop him.

Every Friday night I would attack Oldham with the voracity of youth. Now, I know you'll be saying to yourselves, 'Oldham! It's just a little town stuck between Lancashire and Yorkshire!' This is true, but in the early sixties there were so many pubs down the main street that you couldn't have half a pint in each and still be sober by the time you reached the end of the street. There must have been at least 16 pubs. Each hostelry would have a band pumping out rock'n'roll, and a lot of bands played in Oldham before they were famous – The Beatles, Gerry Marsden, The Foremost, The Chants (who later became The Real Thing), The Merseybeats and many more. They all played the pubs and as you walked along you could hear the different sounds spilling out onto the street, creating an atmosphere of great excitement.

When Tommy and I first bumped into each other in the middle of all this, he was always with his friend Albert. The thing I immediately noticed about Tommy was his resemblance to a singer who was a huge hit in the fifties, Ronnie Carroll. He had many hit records and Tommy was the spitting image of him. As a young man Tommy was exceptionally good looking and when it came to getting attention from the girls in the pubs he had no problem. I never realized that he was, in fact, very shy.

I was a little jealous of all this attention from girls because I was small with funny hair and gappy teeth. (My mother used to be worried that I would become a dwarf!) This did nothing for my feelings of self-worth.

Tommy seemed to have everything going for him, whereas I seemed to have nothing. He was also a bit of a poser. His clothes were immaculate – I don't think I ever saw Tommy scruffy; even his overalls at work had ironed creases down the front! Mine were full of holes and hanging together with dirt; Tommy's were washed and ironed every week. He also owned his own car, a pretty unique thing in those days. It was his access to wheels that gave him away as a bit of a show-off. It was a little white Mini with black-and-white racing stripes down the sides, two aerials and about six headlamps. This type of car wasn't usually seen in Oldham, but Tommy had to have one. Boy, what a poser!

When I took on the weekend residency drumming, Tommy and his mates would come and watch me, then leave at about ten o'clock to go to the Candlelight Club. It was horrendous for me, because every time I started one of my big closing numbers, 'A Whiter Shade Of Pale', they would start to laugh and shout across at me as they left. They knew that I would have preferred to join them rather than be stuck finishing off my act in a little dingy club. That job didn't last long.

Once we'd decided to create our own act, we started rehearsing with vigour and commitment. The only problem was Tommy. Although he had a great voice, when he sang he stood there like a rabbit caught in a car's headlights on the M1, almost frozen to the spot. I could see the mirror idea didn't appeal to him at all. He caused a big fuss, and for a moment I thought our double act had ended as quickly as it had begun, but eventually he bit the bullet and there was no stopping him. His vanity took over. (I know he would deny it, but he was that vain, he used to park in Lovers' Lane on his own.) Singing to himself in the mirror, he became a natural, loving every minute of it.

Now that we thought we had a brilliant act, it wasn't long before we were ready to go out into the clubs and get some bookings. In actual fact, our performance was no good at all – we were absolutely terrible. We didn't think so at the time, but we found out soon enough.

My cousin Wally Harper was a larger-than-life character and a professional comic, actually a very good one. There are many acts in show business who should have been big stars but never got the breaks, and he was one of them. If he was on a bill you could guarantee that no one could follow him. He was too strong an act.

He had many different styles through the years, including a ventriloquist act, where he would work a black doll and a white doll together. The black and white dolls would call each other names and it was very funny. You couldn't do an act like that today because it would be in danger of being classed as racist, though at the time there was nothing unkind meant by it.

Wally would try anything once and at one time in his long career he did an act with a palomino pony, training it to perform all sorts of tricks. He and his pony got a booking to appear for a week in a huge nightclub, but Wally refused to do it because they wouldn't give the pony a dressing room of its own.

Wally also performed in a circus for a year and eventually ended up as an impressionist. It was whilst he was working this act that he came into our lives one Monday morning. Tommy and I were hard at work at Bodens when I felt a tap on my shoulder. I looked up and there was Wally. He looked a million dollars in his camel-hair overcoat and mohair suit.

'What are you doing this cr*p for?' he said. He always had a way with words.

'It's my job! And what about saying hello first?' I answered.

'Where's our Tommy?' he continued. He always called him 'our Tommy' even though they weren't related.

'Tommy!' I shouted over to him. 'Wally's here!'

Tommy came over and shook hands with Wally. 'Hiya, Wally,' he said, 'how are you doing?'

'I'm doing fantastic,' he replied, 'not like you two.'

'What do you mean?' Tommy answered back a little angrily.

'Well,' Wally continued, 'look at you both, mutually covered in grease and mess, working in this rubbish place. With voices like yours you should be professional like me. You work 12 hours a day just to make ends meet, and I work two hours a night and live well.'

'But you're a good act,' I answered, feeling a little envious of him.

'Look,' he said, 'this weekend is Easter weekend and I'm working in Wales, and they need another act. All you have to do is four shows, and you'll get 12 quid.'

We finally agreed to take the time off work and do the shows, but it turned out to be a complete disaster. At each of the four clubs we were told in no uncertain terms to get out because we were supposedly rubbish – or to put it in their terms, 'Get out of here, you're a pile of sh*t!' They paid us off with a couple of quid, but it wasn't just our pride that took a bit of a knocking that weekend. We ended up with less cash than we'd started with.

On the way home, Tommy and I stopped in a lay-by feeling as if we were the worst performers who had ever graced a stage. With the lack of ready money in mind,

Tommy started sifting through the ashtray in the car to see if there were any dog-ends left that we could smoke.

'Do you think we should pack it all in, Tommy, and go back to welding?' I asked, as he continued his fervent search for the elusive butt.

Tommy didn't answer for a second or two, then suddenly he lifted his head beaming from the ashtray, and in his hand was a half-smoked cigarette. There were enough puffs left in it for the two of us. He lit the cigarette and slowly inhaled the smoke with an aristocratic air. 'No, Bobby, I don't,' he said eventually. 'We've only just started and so we can only get better.'

'Yes, but what if we don't?' I questioned him, looking longingly at the now dwindling cigarette he was still clutching in his fingers.

'We will, Bobby,' he assured me, and finally handed me the cigarette. 'We just have to try harder.' Tommy has always had a positive attitude and this is what pulled us through many a difficult time. He finished his smoke and we set off again for home, trying to put the terrible weekend behind us.

The humiliation of the Welsh experience created a new drive and determination to work at the act and refine its possibilities. Encouraged by Tommy, we still hammered on the door of any club around for an opportunity to perform, and we started to get new bookings in local venues. Sometimes the audience liked us, and when that happened it was an indescribable feeling. It sent me high as a kite, as if I had conquered the world. When they didn't like us, it made me want to see the ground below my feet open up and swallow me whole, but we were learning – fast.

Local clubs provided the perfect environment for us

to try out our musical material; the trouble was with the musicians. Many of the ones who backed the visiting acts were terrible and could hardly read the music. Not all were like this, I hasten to add, but there were quite a few. The musicians usually consisted of an organist and a drummer, although if the club was rich they might also have a bass player too, but this was rare. These musicians had been playing at the club for centuries, so they knew every member of the audience and were friends with most of them. If a singer went to the club, he could be the best singer in the world, but if the organist was bad and couldn't play his music, the audience would still blame the crooner. The organist was their friend and imagined he was the best.

On one of our early dates, Tommy and I turned up at a club somewhere in Yorkshire and made our way to the dressing room. Ordering two pints from the bar, we started getting ready to go on stage. The concert secretary came in and told us we could expect to be on in half an hour.

'But we haven't given our music to the organist or drummer yet,' I explained.

'We don't have a drummer,' he retorted. 'Don't need one!'

'Why's that?' Tommy asked, in a tone that really said, 'Here we go.'

'Because Harry is the best organist you'll ever hear.'

'Oh right,' I said sarcastically. 'We can't wait to meet him.'

Turns (the rather charmless name used by club committees for performers) apparently asked to be booked back because they had enjoyed Harry's playing so much, the secretary confidently told us. He walked out of the door, leaving us to look at each other in the silence, with similar thoughts floating through our minds.

About 10 minutes later there was a knock on the door. 'Come in!' we shouted.

No response. Another knock. 'Come in!' we bellowed in unison. Slowly the door opened and an elderly man walked in. He was followed by an elderly lady, who was holding the man's arm. His other hand held a white stick. The man was clearly blind.

'Hello,' said Tommy gently. 'Can we help you?'

'Hello,' the guy replied, holding out his hand in the opposite direction from where Tommy was standing. 'I'm your organist.'

I could see Tommy's eyes widen in anxiety and we stared at each other, wondering what to say next. Tommy was the first one with the courage to speak up. 'That's nice, sir. The only problem is that we have music for the 10 numbers we sing.'

'Oh, don't worry about that,' smiled Harry. 'I'll play your music all right. Just tell me what order the songs go in. You see, I have my wife beside me at all times. She's a little deaf, but it doesn't bother her too much.'

After Harry and his wife had gone, Tommy and I stood looking at each other and I thought of the three monkeys. See no evil, hear no evil … was any noise likely to come out of Harry's organ, or would we be miming?

'Well, it might be OK. We might just get away with it,' Tommy suggested, breaking the silence. I smiled back, but to be honest I think I had serious doubts that we would even get through the first number.

It was time for us to go on and the concert chairman announced our name. Harry the organist struck up our play-on music and it was almost recognizable. Tommy and I glanced optimistically at each other and bounded out onto the wooden platform they loosely called a 'stage'.

We arrived in front of the audience and burst into our first tune, then instantly realized that something was seriously wrong. Harry was playing a different song from the one that we were singing. It was obvious that his wife had put the music in the wrong order – but how was he playing anyway?

Midstream, and still trying to smile at the audience, we looked across at Harry's little wooden box at the side of the stage, where an unbelievable sight met our eyes. Harry's elderly wife was crouched under the organ, with her head poking up by his bench. This enabled her to read the music and tell Harry which chords to play. She was doing this with all the passion and commitment of a schoolteacher barking orders during a PE lesson. She couldn't be seen by the audience because of a curtain which had been taped around the bottom of the organ. I gave Tommy a 'don't ask me why' gaze across the stage as we struggled to continue.

Whatever the reason for the mix-up, it wouldn't help Tommy and I as we swayed to a tune neither of us recognized, looking like a pair of lemons. We could see the audience weren't happy either, and after a few unsettled moments the shouting began. The comments screamed above the cacophony squarely pinned the blame on us for the pitiful noise emanating from the platform.

I ran quickly over to Harry and stopped him by placing my hand on his shoulder. The wind organ subsided like an exhausted set of bagpipes and his wife slid back into her hiding place as I rearranged our music in the correct order. Giving 'Mrs Harry' a nod to tell her to proceed, I dashed back to the centre of the stage where Tommy was trying to pretend that everything was under control.

Selling our best, show-stopping numbers with the ferocity of animal trainers, we succeeded in winning our audience back and eventually finished our spot with more than a little relief. Arriving back at the dressing room, we found the concert chairman waiting for us.

'My, you were lucky there, boys,' he announced.

'I know,' chuckled Tommy with an obvious air of reprieve about him.

'If it hadn't been for Harry and his wife's quick thinking,' the chairman continued, 'you'd have gone down like a lead balloon.'

Encouraged by our good performance against all odds, we pressed on mercilessly and tried to think of ways to improve our image. We picked a new name that we thought was cool and went to the tailors in Oldham to have two blazers made with badges depicting our new name. Tommy was Stevie Rhythm and I was Bobby Rhythm. We proudly wore our new outfits and felt like a million dollars. We would stand at the bar before a show, preening ourselves and talking grandly about future prospects.

Needless to say, neither the name nor the outfits lasted long and we quickly changed to calling ourselves the Sherrel Brothers. We bought some more stage clothes and were now ready to take the world by storm. It was 15 years before it even started to rain.

CHAPTER FIVE

DOING THE ROUNDS

The interminable touring of working men's clubs is known in show-business terminology as 'doing the rounds'. Reminiscent of a milkman doing his daily deliveries, these 'rounds' would take place over a number of years, but an act could only expect to make a return visit to the same club every six months or so. That is, if they could get the booking in the first place! Most acts, or turns, considered these rounds as the necessary stepping stones to stardom. Not only was there a chance that an agent would spot you in one of these 'hunting grounds', but you had the chance to hone and polish your act while you waited for the day of the big break to arrive. Sadly, for most that day never came. Some were content to make a tidy living out of what they could get on the circuit, but others would lose hope and abandon ship. As far as Bobby and Tommy were concerned, their drive and determination were enormous. For them, says Tommy, there was only one way to go – forward.

Auditions are not just confined to actors in the world of 'legitimate' theatre. With our new singing act we knew that the only way to push ahead into the business was to go around the working men's clubs giving auditions and selling ourselves. The only problem was that our touting for business was done live in front of an audience! We used to go in and ask the concert secretary, the man who was in charge of booking the entertainment, if we could get up and sing between the other acts. Some of them agreed and willingly allowed us to show what we could do, but many were power crazy.

These ones would usually be the bookers for little working men's clubs seating about 100 people, and in their own minds they must have thought they were budding Bernard Delfonts. They would treat us like dirt and put us down as much as possible, but we had to get started somehow and this seemed the only way. Every Saturday and Sunday we would tour the clubs, begging the concert secretary to let us get up and sing. We would manage about three clubs a night in the hope that we could persuade the 'little Hitlers' to book us for a later week.

Eventually our perseverance paid off and we got a booking at a little club in Burnley, Lancashire, called The 77 Club. This was to be our first real professional appearance, and we were even going to get paid for it! We set off to the club full of eagerness and anticipation, but as we got nearer I started to feel incredibly nervous. As my stomach started to roll I noticed that Bobby didn't seem to be worried at all. By the time we arrived my mind was filled with dread.

Walking into the club, I noticed a guy was already on stage rehearsing his songs with the band. His confidence and control only made my own insecurities increase, and I feared I was losing my bottle altogether. The singer was so cool, he was obviously the top of the bill and from the back of the auditorium he looked familiar. As we got closer to the stage I saw that it was Vince Hill, a huge star with many hits to his name, and a consummate professional – and here was I, looking up at him from the auditorium, a shaking welder who thought he could sing. The butterflies in my stomach were now flying around in my throat. I convinced myself I could never be that good and started to feel sick.

The manager of the club introduced us to Vince and I was overawed. This was our first proper date and we were expected to work alongside a man of this calibre, the first star I had ever met. We said our smiling hellos to Vince and disappeared quickly into our little hole of a dressing room. Bobby and I hung up our costumes, talked about the act and heard the audience arrive, while my nerves continued with a vengeance. I was so scared that I had to concentrate on going over and over the song lyrics in order to stop my hands trembling. I was convinced that my fear would mean that when I eventually got out there on stage I would open my mouth and nothing would come out!

We watched the clock as each interminable minute clicked by, and then the moment of truth came: it was time for us to go on stage. I was filled with the most overwhelming terror I had ever known, and it didn't help seeing Bobby so obviously excited and impatiently ready to 'storm them'. I was afraid of letting him down, of letting myself down, and of making us look like idiots in front of everybody. Suddenly the compere started to announce us.

'I'm going to be sick!' I hissed at Bobby.

He looked at me as if I had lost my mind. 'You can't be sick now,' he said, with no sympathy in his voice, 'we're on!'

'I can't help it!' I said, feeling my stomach starting to

heave. Desperately I looked around for a sink or something, but there was nothing.

'Do it behind that curtain,' Bobby said, pointing to a curtain at the back of the dressing room.

I ran towards the curtain and started to be sick for Britain. The compere had announced us and left the stage. The audience was just sitting there waiting for us to come on. Eventually I finished vomiting and Bobby dragged his green-looking partner on stage. How I got through it I shall never know, but we seemed to do all right. When we came off the compere said, 'That was a nice opener, keeping them waiting.' Little did he know that not only was I being sick, but if there had been an outside door I wouldn't have gone on stage at all!

It took a long time for me to get rid of my stage nerves, but eventually they eased and I was pleased to hear that some of my fellow professionals suffered in the same way. The more we performed, the less my nerves played up, and despite the mess we left the dressing room in, we started to get more bookings.

Through our work in the clubs during the late seventies we met a guy named Ronnie Lewis and he became a good friend. He managed to get us bookings in Stockport, about 15 miles from Oldham, which meant that we were starting to spread our wings as an act. We had also changed our name a few times and were now called The Harper Bros.

It was in Stockport one night that, unbeknown to us, there was an agent in the house. It was a good job that we didn't know who he was or where he was from, as it would probably have been difficult not to perform our whole act focused towards him. After we had finished our set, this man called us over to join him at his table for a drink.

Dave Morris looked every inch the agent. He sat there with a huge cigar in his mouth, gold bracelets on his wrists, and a very expensive suit. He told us he was from London and that he wanted to manage us. We were dumbfounded. This was our chance. Here was a guy who was obviously a big wheel in London and he wanted us on his books. He told us he had plans for us and that the first thing we must do was to finish working in the factory and become professional entertainers. We looked at each other, wondering if this was too good to be true.

We made arrangements to go down to London the following week and sign contracts with him. We went home that night with our heads in the clouds. Was it all a dream? After we had discussed our exciting news with our wives, we all decided to give it a go. This was what we had been waiting for, so we certainly couldn't let it slip away now.

Knowing nothing about the real business side of the profession, we ignorantly signed Dave Morris's contract a week later, giving him sole representation of our act. He instantly gave us two bookings in Newcastle, promised there would be plenty more and told us to go back home and give up our day jobs.

We marched into work the following day and proudly told the foreman what we had decided to do. He didn't believe us at first and maybe I detected a spark of jealousy in the look on his face. Waving goodbye to our workmates, we swept out through the grimy doors with a feeling that we were on our way to heaven. We had escaped at last, and now the world would see what we were made of. Welders today, stars tomorrow.

The Newcastle bookings came and went and then … just silence. We contacted our new agent and he reassured us with many promises, but we didn't get another booking off him. Each day we waited anxiously, hoping to hear, and each day we became more and more depressed. With no wages coming in, we started to find it hard going. It seemed as if we had made the biggest mistake of our lives.

Maybe the humiliating thought of having to go back to the foreman with our tails between our legs after such a grand exit motivated us to make it work somehow. Going back to our original plan of forcing auditions in the working men's clubs seemed the best way forward, as well as trying to find a little temporary work to do during the day. We had to bring the money in somehow. I found Bobby and myself a few odd jobs, including replacing loose slates on people's roofs, and I even got us employment at a kennels. There we would be, cleaning up dog muck and rehearsing our act at the same time. I often wondered what the dogs might have said about the noise had they been able to speak.

We did this for many months and spread our name around, and eventually bookings started to roll in again. At long last our diary was full and we stopped our day jobs once more. The rehearsals at the dog pound must have helped, for the act felt better than before and our confidence reigned supreme as we realized that we had at last become the fully fledged professional performers we had always dreamt of being. After our bad experience with Dave, we remained wary of signing up to one particular agent, but several were now booking us and the world was looking rosy.

By this time Bobby and I were doing a little comedy too – and when I say a little, I mean a little. We would do a song and maybe tell one gag before the next song. We weren't real comedians, we were an act that just played with a laugh or two in order to fill the gaps. Deciding to change our name once again, we came up with Cannon and Ball.

One agent from Oldham saw us around this time and started to get us some good gigs. He must have seen our potential and realized that what was missing was a little hardening up. He told us that we should go over into the Yorkshire working men's clubs to improve our act. Perhaps he wasn't exactly breaking into a sweat to keep hold of us as an act after all, because the Yorkshire working men's clubs had a reputation for being very hard. It was possible that after one appearance there you might never be seen again. If you weren't going down too well with the audience, you soon knew about it – about two minutes into your act, to be precise!

The audience would boo and the concert secretary would just tell you to leave and give you half the money you were booked to appear for. This was called being 'paid off'. It was to happen to Bobby and me four times over the next few months, and was just as soul destroying every time. We would walk away from each club with our confidence in tatters, until we started to talk about it, get angry, blame the audience and regain our self-respect. I suppose the old saying in show business that if you've never been paid off then you aren't a professional act kept our morale high on these occasions.

Despite the rumours we'd heard, we decided to take the agent's advice and made our way over the border into Yorkshire. The rumours were right. The clubs were hard. It was at a club in a place called Glasshoughton that we first encountered the nightmare of being paid off, but not in a way we could have expected. We were booked to work Sunday lunchtime and Sunday night. This was known as getting a 'noon and nighter'. The men would come in at lunchtime and watch the act, and if it was any good then they would bring their wives along in the evening. If the act was no good they wouldn't return and the concert secretary would be extremely annoyed at having lost the bar revenue.

We arrived at Glasshoughton at midday and went into the little backstage space they called a dressing room. When the lunchtime audience arrived it seemed strange because it was so quiet; there wasn't the usual hustle and bustle and shouts that we had grown to expect. I peeked out of our door to see what was going on and couldn't believe my eyes. There they were, all these guys, each one sitting still with a vegetable on the table in front of him. Seeing each of these burly-looking blokes displaying a different piece of greengrocery made me laugh because it was such a funny picture. It felt as if we were working in a market rather than a place of entertainment.

I called Bobby over to have a look and we burst into hysterics. We couldn't stop laughing, until it was time for us to perform and we had to fight to compose ourselves. When we got on stage my first words of introduction were, 'Well, I see you've all just come off your allotments with your little turnips and carrots. At least it's better than taking the wife out!'

There was a deathly hush. They just looked at us as if we had committed a murder. We had obviously deeply offended them somehow, but we managed to continue the act. We walked off stage to the sound of our own footsteps. When we got back to the dressing room the committee was waiting for us.

'Well, there was no need for that!' a little guy in a flat cap said.

'For what?' I pretended.

'You two,' he continued in his thick Yorkshire accent, 'takin' mickey outta lads and their vegetables.'

'It was only a joke,' Bobby replied.

'Well, I'll tell thee 'ow much of a joke it is!' he said, his voice starting to get louder. 'Thee't being paid off, thee. Thee'll be only getting half thi money.'

'It was only a joke about their vegetables,' I said, trying to make him understand, but he wasn't having any of it.

'Tha said,' he continued, 'that our members had brought their vegetables t'club instead of their wives, and what tha doesn't know is that they do love their vegetables more than their wives, particularly today.'

'Why? What's so special about today?' asked Bobby.

'What's so special about today?' the man replied, almost losing his false teeth. 'It's vegetable prize-giving day!'

'Oh sorry,' I said, 'we didn't know.'

'Well, it's too late to be sorry now,' he shot back. 'Thee'll just have to leave t'club.'

It was unbelievable; it was laughable, but we were goners. The problem we faced now was the fact that the only way to get out of the club was to walk through the audience and out of the front door. We knew how much they hated us now, but we had to face them. Perhaps some of the prize vegetables would even be thrown in our direction!

We got our gear together, took a deep breath, opened the door and started to walk though the club. Suddenly all the audience started to boo. It seemed like the longest walk of my life. I looked back at Bobby and he was following me with his head bowed. It was so humiliating. They carried on booing us until we'd left the club. We sat outside in the car, numb and in silence. We were so embarrassed. We felt like the worst act in the world and had lost a whole day's money as well. We were depending on the extra income, and it took us quite a while to get over both the financial and emotional shock of that day.

Another time, we were sacked after being booked to work at one of the biggest working men's clubs in Sheffield. The Dial House was huge and was one of the few clubs that had electric curtains. If an act got a booking there it was a prestigious thing. We were excited to get the chance to show our mettle and thrilled to see that the place was packed. They had about three acts going on in turn and Bobby and I were the first ones to appear. We dashed on stage and started our performance, but halfway through our second number the curtains started to close. We thought they must be broken, so we stepped forward in front of them. The curtains started to open again, so we moved back, further up the stage. Then they started to close again, so we moved forward. The audience sat there open mouthed, unable to believe what they were seeing. This carried on all the way though the act.

When we came off the concert secretary was waiting for us. 'I'm paying you off,' he said. 'You're no good.'

'It's not our fault that the curtains are broken!' I replied.

'They're not broken,' he said. 'I've been trying to close them on you for the last half hour.'

We started to laugh because we could see the funny side of it. There we were, dodging the curtains because we thought they were broken, and he'd been trying to catch us behind the curtains so that he could pull us off. Our laughter only aroused his anger even more, however, and once again we left a club with our tails between our legs. Many years later the club was rebuilt. We were doing our own TV series by then, and we got a letter from the same man asking us to open the new club. We wrote a letter back saying, 'Not unless you fix the broken curtains.' Needless to say, we weren't invited back.

The Yorkshire club scene became our working place and, although it was hard, it taught us how to work audiences properly. It was an invaluable experience to be able to test everything out on stage in front of a live audience which needed to be won over. I think this is where some TV comedy can sometimes fall foul – the laughs can't always be tested in the same way and a programme can often end up pretty flat as a result. Doing those clubs taught us discipline and timing as an act. When the laugh didn't come we would cut the gag the next time, but when something went wrong it often got a greater laugh than a planned gag, so we kept it in. I still feel it's a great training ground for comedians and if anybody came to me today and said they wanted to be a comic, then I would tell them to forget the comedy rooms and perform in the working men's clubs. You really will come away with an act that can survive anywhere.

The appeal of Cannon and Ball stretched more widely, and we seemed to be spending more time in the car than actually appearing on stage. Gigs in Scotland

and Wales soon beckoned, and one particular club in the Northeast will never be forgotten, as we were lucky to escape with our lives. Now, when we reminisce about old times, we laugh about it. We didn't at the time, believe me.

We had stormed them that night and came off the stage to the sound of the audience shouting for more. In the Northeast that's good! Jealousy amongst colleagues in the business, however, is deadly. No sooner had we got back into the dressing room than the door burst open and the compere came in. We could still hear the audience shouting for us.

'Are you going back on?' he asked.

Bobby and I looked at each other, realizing that we didn't have any more material. We had sung every song we knew and told every joke we had. There was nothing else we could do. 'No,' I replied, 'we don't have anything else to give them. We've used all our material.'

In the background we could still hear the audience shouting for more. 'So you're not going back on, then,' the compere said, his tone changing from friendly to slightly aggressive.

I looked at Bobby and I could see his face changing, because Bobby was also aggressive and he hadn't liked the compere from the moment he had met him. 'Hey, cock!' Bobby shouted. 'Tommy's told you once we haven't enough material, so stop asking!'

The compere looked at Bobby as if he was going to hit him. Bobby clearly hoped he would, but he backed down and opted for revenge of an even greater nature instead. He just stomped out of the room, banging the door behind him and leaving us in stunned silence. For a moment Bobby and I just stood there looking at each other, then we burst out laughing. Our laughter suddenly stopped when we heard the audience cheer. The compere had gone back on stage and the crowd would now expect us to follow him and entertain them some more.

'Ladies and gentlemen,' we heard the compere announce, 'I've had a word with the boys about entertaining us some more, but they've just told me that they're not going to do that. Because they said you've been a bad audience and they aren't getting enough money anyway. So that's the end of the concert. Goodnight.' With that he walked off. The audience suddenly changed from cheering us to booing us. We could hear them from our dressing room, baying like dogs for our blood.

I was furious and started to go out of the door to find the compere and give him a piece of my mind, but Bobby stopped me. 'Don't go out there, you'll get lynched,' he said, pulling me back into the room.

I agreed and we decided to wait until the audience had calmed down before sneaking out of the back door. I would run into the compere some other time, I figured, and then he would really know what it was like to be lynched!

After about 30 minutes the booing stopped and the club seemed quiet at last. I sneaked to the side of the stage and peeked through the curtains. The club was empty apart from a couple of bar staff cleaning up. This was our chance to get away. We collected our things together and made for the back door like thieves in the night, opened the exit and ran for the car. We had just got in and closed the doors when a gang of tough guys came round the corner. One of them spotted us and shouted, 'There they are!' and started to run towards us. Bobby and I went into panic mode, locking the doors as quickly as possible, and I turned the key in the ignition to get the motor started. Just our luck, it wouldn't start. It was like a scene from a film.

The old car had been having trouble starting for a while. Sometimes it did and sometimes it didn't. Typically it decided it wasn't going to start that night, just when we needed it most. The gang was now all around the car, shouting abuse at us and banging on the windows. Bobby was yelling at me, 'Get it started! Get it started!' I was turning the key and banging my foot down on the accelerator, but all it would do was choke out a pitiful moan. Suddenly the gang decided they were going to get it moving themselves by the unusual method of turning the vehicle over onto its side.

We slid across our seats as we felt them starting to lift the wheels off the ground. Panic filled me as I envisaged the end both of us and my beloved car. I had visions of myself hanging upside down inside while my head was kicked in. Frantically I pulled and pushed every knob and lever I could, but it must have been the motion of the tipping car that caused the engine to kick in suddenly and roar into life. I slammed it into gear and we sped away, leaving the gang rolling around on the ground in a cloud of dust. Bobby and I didn't speak for at least 10 minutes, until our sense of relief caused us to laugh. I didn't know if I had run any of them over, but I have to tell you that at that moment I couldn't have cared less. Although the lifting of the car started the engine, I don't recommend this method today!

CHAPTER SIX

CURRY FOR SUPPER

The incident with the car ensured that Bobby's hair stood on end even more than usual. Aggressive fighter as he was, he admits to being a real coward inside when it came to a complete gang! Bobby's memories of the days in the clubs are looked back on with great fondness. Where else could he have gained the insight and experience that would eventually turn two guys from Oldham into one of the biggest and most successful double acts in the country? While the clubs would lay the foundations of professional experience essential to success, however, nothing could prepare them emotionally for the heady days of stardom which were to follow.

An Indian restaurant in Oldham called Shafi's was a strange place to perform, especially with the heavy fragrance of tikka masala hanging in the air. With a little stage in the corner of the room, a pianist and a drummer, Shafi would book an act to entertain his diners whilst their food was being prepared. It must have been one of the first Indian restaurants in the north and we agreed to try out our act there for one night. After our 40 minutes, Shafi told us that he'd liked us so much he wanted to book us regularly once a week. He offered us

£3 a night and a free curry, which was good news until he told us which night he wanted us: Friday.

Friday was the worst night of the week for any act, simply because the crowds got plastered more quickly after the week's work was over. We accepted Shafi's offer anyway, because we thought it would make the act even tighter and it meant regular pay.

Let me tell you, no money in the world could compensate for what we went through. We would go on stage at about 11.30, just in time for the drunks to start arriving. Whilst we were singing, all the local lads who had been drinking around the town would pile into the restaurant for their usual cheap meal. It was pointless trying to sing above the noise, but we carried on anyway. We needed the money, and the curry wasn't too bad. We always managed to finish just as the plates and glasses started flying.

The trip down to London to sign contracts with the agent Dave Morris was a wonderful day for me. Of course it was to prove a complete waste of time, but on that day our hopes were high and I felt I was starting out on the adventure of my life. I had never been to London before, so for me it was the start of the big time. It was all incredibly exciting – the black cabs, the guards outside Buckingham Palace, the hustle and bustle of people going about their daily lives. It was magical and I loved it. Strangely enough, later on in life I grew to hate it.

The winter of 1978 when we signed on the dotted line was a particularly bad one and the long journey back home was extremely cold; even the railway tracks froze over. The train came to a stop and we were told that the heating system had packed up. We sat there and watched frost start to appear on the inside of the windows. People wrapped newspaper around themselves to try and keep warm. It was horrendous, really, but this didn't bother Tommy and me – we were too high. Everybody in the carriage was moaning and shivering, but Tommy and I were laughing our heads off and singing popular songs. The other passengers must have thought we were crazy. What they didn't know was that we had a million-dollar contract in our pockets.

It turned out, of course, that Dave's piece of paper was only worth about £100 for the two gigs he arranged for us, but our hopes stayed high. Maybe there were other opportunities for us just around the corner. We were ready to try anything, even television if we could find a way to get on it.

At a time when television sets were still considered a luxury, I remember the day my mother and father bought one. Well, they didn't strictly buy it – it was rented. It was a Grundig 12-inch black-and-white set, and the year was 1958. When it arrived we all sat around it and stared at the test card for at least an hour. Programmes were only broadcast a few hours a day then, mainly in the evenings between six and ten o'clock. The first advert I saw blew my mind. It showed two bottles of beer set in a boxing ring. One of the bottles was Mackinson's Stout and the other was just ordinary beer. The bottles danced around the ring for a while and then started to box. The Mackinson won and the referee raised the bottle's arms as the winner. It really had an effect on me and I can still see it all clearly in my mind today.

Television in those days was so simple and family orientated, but it never played a big part in my childhood and this feeling was to continue. I only occasionally watched it. My time seemed to be taken up with other things, and I found I was too active just to sit down for hours in front of a tiny screen. What I did see made a big impression on me, however, particularly when it came to light entertainment. Although I enjoyed programmes like *Top of the Pops*, a sci-fi series called *The Outer Limits*, and my favourite cowboy drama, *The High Chaparral*, I was particularly drawn to the comedy programmes. There were some great comics, my favourite being Max Wall. Whenever he was on I would be glued to the set and when he started to do his funny walks I would just roll off the settee with laughter. I found him so funny and never thought that later I would get the chance to meet him. Funnily enough, I refused that opportunity, afraid that the real Max Wall would spoil the image of a comedy genius I had built up in my mind.

Comics like Tommy Cooper, Fred Emney and Morecambe and Wise ruled the roost as far as I was concerned, and whatever programmes these people were appearing on I would watch. Although I loved comics, however, I never felt it was possible for me to become one. I was content to throw out a gag between songs, and this was the format we used when we auditioned for *Opportunity Knocks*.

We were 'filling in' at the dog kennels when we got a letter saying that we had been accepted to take part in this new TV talent show. We had actually auditioned 12 months earlier, but as we hadn't heard anything we had given up waiting. Lots of new acts had appeared on the show and when they did, their profile went up, so it was the obvious thing for any act to apply for. It didn't actually matter whether you won or not – once you had appeared on television you could charge a higher fee for your live gigs. It also opened the door for summer seasons, pantomimes and other, bigger clubs, so maybe we would strike lucky.

The advert in the local paper was irresistible. Thames Television were holding auditions at a hotel in Manchester and there was an open invitation for acts to come along. When we arrived it was incredibly busy, and I'm sure the hotel management were very surprised at all the activity buzzing around them. Singers, comics, jugglers, magicians – all kinds of performers jostled each other as we entered the dreaded audition room.

One by one we stood in front of Hughie Green and Royston Mayo, the producer. Our turn came and we proceeded to try to give our best in the silence – very difficult for a double act relying on some kind of audience response! We finished our little spot to the applause of two people, Hughie Green and Royston Mayo. The other acts weren't going to clap, were they? We were told that we would receive notice in the post whether we had passed the audition or not. The old saying, 'Don't ring us, we'll ring you,' is absolutely true.

Les Dawson also auditioned that day and he was terrific. Les got through the auditions without any problems and went on to become one of this country's best-loved stars. He just sat at his piano and played as only he could and the room full of other performers, who are always the hardest people to please, just laughed and laughed. Later on in life we became close friends and it was a great loss to comedy when he left us.

As we stood amongst the kennels with the Thames Television letter in our hands, a strange thing happened. My heart sank and my confidence started to deflate. We had made it through the audition, been asked to appear on the programme, and now I doubted our ability. I mulled over what would be involved as I realized that it was one thing to perform to an audience, but quite a different matter to try to entertain with four cameras stuck up your nose. Not only that, but the cameras would be between us and the audience and I just didn't think we could bridge the gap. Our inexperience in this matter soon became obvious when we arrived at the television centre a few weeks later.

My impression on seeing the inside of a television studio for the first time was that it had a very clinical atmosphere and was certainly not what I had expected. I expected a buzz, a hive of creativity, but instead all I found were people going around doing jobs just like in everyday life. The dressing rooms were also very sterile. Ours felt very much like a doctor's waiting room, not the exciting place I had imagined.

We didn't really get to meet Hughie Green. We only saw him from a distance, but he seemed to be a very powerful person within the realms of TV. The floor manager called us politely from our dressing room, and my top lip started to stick to my gums as we walked down the corridor and onto the studio floor. We were carefully positioned in front of the cameras and I wondered how far I would be allowed to move before going out of shot. I hadn't been so nervous since our first club gig several years previously. Feeling like a ventriloquist's dummy, with a false smile stuck on my face to hide the fact that I was petrified, I started to lick my lips and gums constantly. It must have looked as if I had an affliction of some sort.

Once we had finished our performance we went backstage to wait for the results, with polite applause ringing in our ears. This was make-or-break time, we thought, and we must surely win. After the acts had finished their respective spots, they were judged by the 'clapometer', which measured the strength of the audience's applause. Someone somewhere must have invented that name, but they've never admitted it. Our turn came and we watched on the TV monitor as the audience hardly clapped at all and the damn machine scarcely moved. We came last and I was almost in tears from embarrassment. I felt like a complete failure and angry that we had missed our chance of fame and fortune.

A young boy won it. He played drums whilst his father played the organ, and they were called Simon Smith and Father. Although they were an original act, I felt that they were going nowhere because they had little to offer apart from playing nice songs. They would never survive in the tough world of show business and probably didn't even want to be in it anyway, except as a hobby. It seemed to me to be a chance wasted as the British public fell in love with this little boy, while we had been rejected. I felt sorry for him in a way, because once he started to grow into a man he would either pack the business in or become a professional drummer, and there weren't too many drumming stars.

Seeing Simon and his father claim the prize on *Opportunity Knocks* made us set aside any grand thoughts of becoming television stars, but it succeeded in making us even more determined to find our own success elsewhere. Maybe television wasn't for us; our place was probably in the clubs – but first we had to face the dreaded journey back up north, once more with our tails between our legs.

Auditions followed bookings and bookings followed more auditions. We started to keep a log of the clubs we played and the list got longer and longer. As with everything else, there were good places and bad places, and we made a note of them all. When a return booking came we could refer back to our comments to see what had worked and how well we had done. Funnily enough, we seemed to work most of the bad places. I'm not saying that it was all bad clubs, because we would occasionally get a good one and that would make up for the torturously awful nights we suffered.

Some of the hardest battles we fought in the clubs were still with the resident musicians. There were some great musicians in the clubs, but when you got a bad one, they were really bad.

A singer friend of mine, Billy Caruso, sang in the Mario Lanza vein. He had done this particular club before, so he knew how bad the resident player was. He did what most acts would do and just sang the song trying to overcome whatever noise was coming from the accompanist. This was particularly necessary when the organist wasn't even playing what was written on the music, but just making it up as he went along, with singer and organist trying to battle it out between them.

Arriving on stage one night, Billy gave the music to the organist and went on to do his spot. As usual the organist was bluffing his way through and Billy just ignored him and tried his best to blank him out. Halfway through the second song the organist had a heart attack and fell forward onto his keyboard. All that could be heard was a continuous drone coming from the organ. Neither Billy nor the audience noticed that anything was amiss for the whole duration of the song! Eventually someone called an ambulance.

When Billy told me about it I laughed and laughed, because I could just see the picture in my mind. Billy said he wouldn't have noticed at all if it hadn't been for some members of the audience frantically pointing at the organist. Luckily the guy survived and apparently went back to the club, telling people that it was Billy's singing that gave him the heart attack in the first place.

One of the most notorious 'hard' clubs was the Lions Club in Hartlepool. The dressing room wall was covered with graffiti, messages from other acts who had appeared there. In show business language, 'to die the death' means that your act didn't go down well at all. The general mood of the messages on the walls was one of sheer terror. Some were very humorous, though, and would actually lift the readers' spirits, arming them for the battle ahead:

Men have been to the moon
Men have sailed unknown seas
Men have conquered mountains
I died the death here at the Lions Club

Roses are red
Violets are blue
I died on my a*s
Good luck to you!

The band and audience are cr*p
Just wait and see
You're going to die the death
Just like me...

The best one was written next to an arrow on the wall just as you went on stage: 'This way to the Lions Den!' Strangely enough, Tommy and I always did well at the Lions Club. This tells you one of two things: either we had the makings of a good act, or we were abnormal. Take your pick.

We did these clubs for many years, happy with the way the mixture of songs and short gags seemed to work. Acts at that time were required to perform three separate spots, half an hour long, so that the club members could play bingo in between. The incident that changed the format of our act for ever took place at a famous venue called The Batley Variety Club.

The contrast between Batley's and the other clubs was as big as the difference between a palace and a tent. Batley's had a 10-piece orchestra, whereas the clubs we were used to had an organist and a drummer. We also had only one spot to do at Batley's, instead of the three required by the clubs. Batley's provided you with your own dressing room, easy chairs and a TV. In the clubs we would have to share the only changing room with a stack of chairs and the bingo machine. We always felt that we were really only there to support the bingo, but Batley's had a reputation for offering some of the finest entertainers in England. When we were offered a contract there, we knew that we were playing with the best. We weren't 'just another turn' – we were part of a real show.

Topping the bill that week was Frankie Vaughn. As a singing star he was very well liked, particularly amongst the female population. Having been booked in as a comedy-song act for the whole week, we were given a great spot just before the top of the bill. This was a very prestigious slot, and Tommy and I intended to make the most of it. The show would start with the band playing an opening number, then the speciality act would go on, usually a juggler or a balancing act, then the comics, then the top of the bill. Both Tommy and I were very excited about working this club, because we figured that anything could happen. Maybe Frankie might see us and put us on his television show. Maybe an agent would spot us and send us out on the cabaret circuit...

The first night came and we stood at the side of the stage waiting to go on. The 'spec' act finished his few minutes and suddenly we were on stage at Batley's. We did our usual act, singing a song, telling one joke, then singing another song. Before we knew where we were, we had finished. We took our applause and headed back to the dressing room. We were sitting comfortably, thinking we had done all right, when the door opened and the manager of the club walked in.

'What are you doing?' he barked, frowning at us.

'What do you mean?' I asked rather meekly.

'Your stage act!' he said, his voice starting to rise.

Tommy and I looked at each other dumbfounded, because we thought we had done OK. What was wrong? 'We've just done what we normally do,' I replied, hoping that we weren't going to get paid off again.

'Well, let me tell you something,' the manager said, pacing the room. 'I book comics at this club and I booked you two in the belief that you were comics, but you're not. You're two singers pretending to be comics, so you're no good to me. Frankie Vaughn is the singer and I don't want two singers going on before him, I want a comic. You're neither one thing nor the other!'

My heart sank. This could have been our chance to get on the nightclub circuit and we had blown it once again. I felt totally dejected and worthless. We stood there waiting to hear the familiar words of dismissal.

'So I'll tell you what I'm going to do,' the manager continued. 'I'm going to put you on first and book a real comic for the other slot. I won't pay you off, but tomorrow night just sing.' Then he walked out of the room.

We sat there in silence for about five minutes, then Tommy said, 'Bobby, do you want to be a comic or a singer?'

I looked at him, wondering why he had asked such a question. 'A comic,' I replied immediately, not really thinking much about it. Maybe I just wanted a change from being a crooner?

'Right,' he said. 'After this week, when we do a show we're just taking an opening piece of music and a closing piece and we'll do comedy in the middle. That way no one can accuse us of not being comics.'

It wasn't going to be that easy, I thought, but I knew he was right. We had to let go of one aspect and focus on the other. Maybe this was the element that had been missing for so many years, and had prevented us from finding real success? So we decided to be comics, and shook hands on it to reassure ourselves.

We finished off the week at Batley's and left the club rather discouraged, realizing we were unlikely to be invited back, but carrying a new determination for the future nonetheless. Little did we know that it was to be less than two years before we were to return, topping the bill in our own right.

Our handshake on the decision to become a comedy act finally brought about the right name change. 'The Harper Bros' didn't lend itself to comedy. There was a singer Tommy liked called Freddie Cannon, who had brought out a few hit records in the fifties, and Tommy took on his last name, calling himself Tommy Cannon. Now we had the first name for our new act, but we couldn't find a second name to go with it! I know it sounds stupid, but we just didn't think of the obvious choice for quite a while. We tried Cannon and Short; we tried Cannon and Small; we tried all sorts of combinations, but still couldn't find anything we liked. Then one day Tommy suggested Cannon and Ball. I told him to get lost (or words to that effect). There was no way I was going to call myself Mr Ball. The problem was, we had a gig coming up and we needed a name quickly. In the end I agreed to do it just for that time, if I could change it again later. Well, the rest is history.

Armed with our new name and a new act, we set out to show the world that we were the greatest comics who ever lived. It's strange what egos can do! In those days we wore evening suits and did cross-patter with no sign of the Hush Puppies and braces that were to come. Our first booking as Cannon and Ball was in Wales. We were booked to do a few clubs in the Rhondda Valley and figured this was a godsend, because if we died as a comedy act no one would hear about it.

We arrived in Wales and went straight to our digs to unpack. After being shown our tiny rooms we left for the club, feeling deep down that we had made the right decision. Our intuition was proved right when we found that the laughs actually came – but more than that, we got satisfaction from what we were doing. There's nothing like the sound of an audience laughing, and I found that it sent shivers down my spine. I began to believe that I had the best job in the world.

The great success our new offering brought was followed by the trek back to our bed-and-breakfast digs. When we arrived we found that there were six other acts staying too and they were all sitting in the lounge. This wasn't so bad until I discovered that they were all magicians. I realized that the week would be a nightmare because I'm not a lover of magic and I was bound to be inundated with tricks, left, right and centre. Tommy, on the other hand, was a frustrated David Copperfield (he often tried to impress me with magic tricks) and was highly delighted by the unique company surrounding us. As the only non-magician there, I knew I was in for an overdose of prestidigitation.

Amongst the illusionists was Paul Daniels, soon to become a huge star. When I saw him sitting in the lounge I couldn't believe my eyes. Here we were in a little guesthouse in the middle of Wales, and Paul sat there dressed in a padded smoking jacket with a huge book on Merlin tucked under his arm. I pulled his leg something rotten, but Paul wasn't in the least worried, having always been a very confident man.

Another conjurer, Leslie Melville, had a simple but effective act involving himself and a chicken. He would make the chicken do all sorts of tricks and the finale was to make an egg appear from the chicken's bottom. What a classy act! His only problem that week was the fact that the landlady didn't allow animals in the house, so he used to hide the chicken under his bed. Like all magicians, he had concealment down to a fine art. Whenever the landlady passed his door he would sing at the top of his voice to cover up the clucking noise of the hen. He never got caught.

Mealtimes were the worst for me, because I always seemed to be the fall guy. I would be sitting there with my boiled egg in front of me, trying to blank out any thoughts of Mr Melville and his chicken's rear end, only to find that my egg had suddenly disappeared, and then Leslie would make it reappear behind my ear. Quite apart from the interruptions caused to my breakfast, I was worried that one day he would make the egg appear from my bottom as he did with his hen. On the other side of me Paul would be trying to make me levitate, while I looked desperately at Tommy for help, but he was just taken up with the whole thing and loved every minute of it. It was an awful week for me, and by the time we left I had a loathing for anything that looked remotely like a magic trick.

My aversion to all this fooling with magic may also have had something to do with the fact that my personal life was now in turmoil. I had recognized by then that my relationship with my wife Joan had gone steadily downhill. I was too busy working away from home to notice that I was neglecting Joan, while she could never accept my long days away and needed someone at home with her.

My family was very important to me, but it must have been difficult for them to believe this when I was away so much. Robert and Darren were my pride and joy, though I always secretly feared they might get hooked by show business in the same way that I had been. I would honestly look forward to coming home after a week's work and settling into being domesticated again. As Joan had a daytime job, when I wasn't away I would get the kids off to school, spend the day at home, then pick the boys up from the bus stop at the end of the day before going off to my evening gig if I had one. It wasn't enough, though, and I knew deep down that it was virtually impossible to be a normal father in my profession. I just did the best I could.

Joan and I soon split up. I regretted this, wished it hadn't happened, and felt the hurt deep inside. It was difficult to talk to anybody about it, and I used Cannon and Ball each night as an escape from the guilt and pain.

Eventually she found another man and I was devastated. It felt as if this was really the end now. Any hope of restoring our marriage was gone, and I felt strangely alone. My distress turned to hate for the man she now loved, and I hated myself for letting it happen in the first place. Questions rushed round and round my brain constantly. I couldn't sleep, I felt ill, and wondered if I would survive the emotional darkness that enveloped me. I knew I had to let go, stop myself from going mad and somehow walk away from it all. 'After all, what could I do, hundreds of miles from home?' I reasoned to myself.

I continued to see Darren and Robert as much as possible, who by this time were about nine and eleven years old respectively. I was relieved that they were always pleased to see me and, although the tension at home during my visits was unbearable, I still insisted on seeing them every week.

For a long time I couldn't get over the breakdown of my marriage. It left me very depressed and suspicious of women, and I avoided the opposite sex as much as I could. My focus on our career as Cannon and Ball became even more intense and, I suppose, was a type of therapy. The failure in my marriage probably ensured a greater determination to succeed as Cannon and Ball, and helped push my damaged emotions deep down inside. I hoped these emotions would eventually go away. They didn't, of course, and it wasn't until many years later that I was finally able to surrender some of the pain I constantly carried.

CHAPTER SEVEN

JACK THE HAT

After the bad experience at Batley's, and particularly after their failure on Opportunity Knocks, *it isn't surprising that thoughts of real stardom quickly evaporated. Nevertheless, Cannon and Ball became part of the clique of acts regularly seen in the northern clubs, and they considered settling for contentment as the support act. After all, they had gone further in their careers than they had ever thought possible. They were happily making enough money and the buzz it gave them was sufficient to bring satisfaction. Agents were another matter, however, and the need for a manager to look after their administrative, financial and booking affairs was becoming increasingly obvious. Bobby and Tommy had neither the time, the interest nor the experience to deal with all the backstage negotiations that were beginning to gather pace. As Tommy remembers, Cannon and Ball may not have been famous then, but they were certainly in demand.*

The bright neon lights of the nightclub circuit looked very tempting, and they suddenly came within our reach when the agent who had recommended that we try it out the hard way reappeared in our lives one day. Later on this man was to become our manager for the next 20 years. He had seen or heard that we were doing well and was now offering to manage us. He was a big fish around Manchester in those days, so it felt good when he suggested it.

Landing the odd gig in a nightclub was yet another step up the show business ladder, and before long we had said goodbye to the working men's clubs in favour of these late-night venues, which became our main source of work. They were very exciting days, but the gear change was a problem. Instead of being the kings of the working men's clubs, we were now the small boys on a big circuit of luxurious nightclubs where major stars topped the bills. Big names such as Stevie Wonder, Shirley Bassey, The Beach Boys and many other international stars visited frequently and we needed to be as professionally polished as they were.

Not all the nightclubs were like that, and some were very dingy, but most venues carried the esteem of being vehicles for the cream of the entertainment business. We had to prove what we could do, and we did. Our comedy routine seemed to work wonders. We had drastically altered the act, changing from two smartly dressed men doing cross-patter into a clown and a straight man. We never consciously decided who was going to be the comic and who was going to be the straight man – it just happened. I felt I was a natural feed and Bobby was a natural comic. This combination obviously had the makings of a good comedy act and the chemistry between us would lead us to heights we never imagined we could reach.

An early learning period for Bobby and me included the sharp lesson that you mustn't upset the top of the bill. We had been booked to support a big star at a nightclub in Charnock Richard. The star was a guy called

JACK THE HAT

Johnny Ray who had many hit records in the fifties, including songs like 'Cry' and 'Walking My Baby Back Home'. He was a truly international star, but was also the strangest-looking guy for a sex symbol. In the fifties, girls would rush the stage and try to touch him, and they would faint when he sang. He was one of the original teenybopper idols. What made him the unlikeliest sex symbol was that he was very thin, with long, dangly arms. He was also deaf and wore a hearing aid. In those days there were no hearing aids that you could disguise – this was one of the old-fashioned ones which had a piece of wire coming from his ear and disappearing into his top pocket. He also cried when he sang, which made the girls scream even louder.

It was very exciting for me to be on the same bill as Johnny Ray, because I had his records at home and he was the first American star we had worked with. We arrived early at the club on the first night of the week hoping to meet him, but his dressing room was locked and we were told that he didn't see anybody before he went on stage. I wasn't surprised. Many of the big acts had their funny ways and, after all, he was a big star and we were only a small support act.

That night we did one of the best shows of our lives. I would feed Bobby a line and bang, he would be back with the tag. The act ran like oil. At the end the audience went wild for us and we came off to thunderous applause. As we made our exit, we saw Johnny Ray standing in the wings. My heart started pumping, because I was actually going to meet this megastar. With the applause still ringing in my ears, I held my hand out and proudly said, 'Pleased to meet you, Mr Ray.'

He looked at me as if I was the Black Death. If looks could kill, then I would certainly have been dead. He just stared at my hand and then looked me up and down, and with a flick of his head stomped back into his dressing room, slamming the door behind him. I felt about a foot tall.

'What have I done wrong?' I said, turning to Bobby, whose eyes were twinkling. A slight grin formed at the corner of his mouth. 'We've gone down too well. He'll have a job following us now,' he answered, enjoying every minute of it. 'We won't be working with him again!' And he started laughing.

'OK, if that's how he wants it, he can have it that way,' I said, feeling the challenge rise up inside me. 'Tomorrow night we'll do even better.' I had the bit between my teeth, and I wasn't going to let it go. All week we kept storming the audience, and the better we did the more Johnny Ray struggled. Needless to say, he didn't speak to us or say goodbye at the end of the week.

The good thing to come out of it was that the night-club booked us to come back shortly afterwards as top of the bill. So Johnny Ray had done us a favour and didn't even know it. If he had been civil to us we would have toned the act down, but as it was, we made it our goal that week to try and show who was the better act. It's a cruel business.

The seventies had brought a nightclub boom and almost every town had two or three of them. In those days the support acts went on while the audience were still eating, so that by the time the star came on they had finished and could sit back and give the stage their full attention. It was very difficult to entertain against a background of clanging cutlery, slurping soup and waitresses walking back and forth. Thankfully this problem didn't last long for us, because every time Bobby and I went to a club as the support act, we always got a return booking as the top of the bill. We quickly climbed our way up the ladder and our money climbed too. Our first engagements netted us about £100 a week between us. Even after we had paid out our travelling expenses, tax and manager's percentage, we still made more than we had done as welders. We were very pleased.

We had signed a contract with our new manager that paid him 25 per cent of our fee for every gig we did. The percentage was a little high, even for a manager, as most agents at that time took about 15 per cent. An additional agreement was that if ever we reached a fee of £1,000 we would pay him 33 per cent. You're probably thinking that Bobby and I must have been very naive and you'd be right, because we were, and always have been to our own misfortune. We signed the agreement willingly, because even in our wildest dreams we never expected to get £1,000 for doing what we did. We were happy with what we got and just wanted to concentrate on the act, leaving the business side of things to someone else. In fact, it was only a matter of months before the dream of earning £1,000 as a fee came true.

Wooky Hollow was a famous club in Liverpool. We had done the club years before as singers, and now we were going back as comedians. The owner of Wooky Hollow was a giant of a man called Terry Philips. He had won some bodybuilding championships in his time, so he was the kind of guy you didn't argue with. We arrived on Sunday afternoon and rehearsed with the band. When we had finished we started to walk out of the club, only to be confronted by Terry.

'What are you doing?' he asked aggressively.

Bobby and I stood there shaking. 'We've just been rehearsing with the band,' I finally managed to splutter out.

'You've only rehearsed two songs!' Terry said.

'We know, because we're comedians,' Bobby answered, thinking that this would appease the situation.

Terry looked at us both and the atmosphere became very intense. His voice lowered to hardly a whisper. 'Well,' he said, slowly coming closer to us so that we could almost feel his breath. 'I booked you as singers. So you'd better go away and pray that you're funny.'

He walked away, leaving Bobby and me standing speechlessly by the wall. Now we were really on trial. Would we be deemed funny or not? We went outside and got in the car. Bobby was adamant that he wasn't going back. He said that it wasn't worth it and we should go home. I told him we couldn't afford to do that, as we had families and they needed feeding. We should swallow our pride and do the gig. It didn't matter if we died on stage, because at least we would get paid. After a long time spent trying to persuade him he agreed, but I told him that after this week we would never come back unless they paid us £1,000. This seemed impossible, as we were only taking £100 that week.

That night, waiting to go on stage was a nightmare. Sweat was running down my back as I thought about what had happened in the afternoon. What's more, we were in Liverpool, a place renowned for its comics. Even the ordinary people in the streets are funny. They have a natural sense of humour that seems to run right through their everyday lives. We had a lot to live up to that night.

These were the thoughts running through my head as we went on stage. But I had nothing to worry about. The audience were wonderful and they took Bobby and me to their hearts. We felt elated. To be accepted as comics by Liverpool people was an honour in itself. We were certain that Terry would come in and congratulate us, but he just ignored us all week. This made us even more determined never to come back.

At the end of the week we were just going out of the front doors to head home when we spotted Terry Philips. Surely he would congratulate us now? We had gone down a storm every night. We walked past him, but all he said was, 'See you, boys.' We left the club angry and frustrated. We just couldn't understand why he wouldn't acknowledge that we had done well and kept our promise to be funny.

God moves in mysterious ways, however, because 12 months later we got a booking back at the club, only this time they were paying us £1,000. We couldn't believe it. It was the first time we had earned so much money, and our good feelings towards Terry naturally increased. We told our manager that it would be unfair for us to pay him 33 per cent of the £1,000 and he agreed, settling for 25 per cent. We went back to the club to top the bill. Maybe Terry won't remember it, but he did us a favour when he told us we should pray to be funny. It paid off in more ways than one.

Halfway through the week at the club, we were just leaving when a tall guy came up and knelt before us, bowing to the ground. We wondered who it was, and then he got up and we recognized him straightaway. It was one of the legends of show business, Ken Dodd. He had seen our show and this was his way of saying how much he had enjoyed it. Bobby and I were overawed. Here was one of England's greatest comics saying that he had enjoyed *us*. That memory will stay with me until my dying day.

The only difference between us and most of the other bill-toppers was that they were household names and we were unknown outside the nightclub circuit. There were many acts like us, however, who drew their own following even though the general public at that time didn't know them: The Grumbleweeds, Syd and Eddie, who later became Little and Large, and The Black Abbotts, featuring Russ Abbott. The opportunity to show that we were fully able to take such a high position came unexpectedly. We had been booked by a Sheffield club to support a singer called Matt Monroe, who was one of this country's biggest stars. We enjoyed working with such talented people, not least because we knew the club would be full of excited people, which would make them a good audience.

The Fiesta Club in Sheffield was one of the biggest in the country. We arrived and were immediately informed by the manager that Matt Monroe was ill and wouldn't be appearing. We were expected to go on in his place, he said. Panic set in immediately. There were maybe 1,500 people waiting to see a famous singing star, and all they would get was Bobby and me. We were sure they would go berserk. The manager told us not to worry, and promised he would get the compere to break the news well before we went on. This didn't do much to calm our nerves, but at least the audience would know well in advance and would have time to leave if they wanted to. We hoped that at least some of the crowd would stay.

We began to wonder what it would be like to battle against what would be left of rows of bitterly disappointed people, and prepared ourselves as best we could. The compere asked us if we were ready. We told him that we were as ready as we would ever be and made our way to the side of the stage, waiting in dread for our cue.

The compere went on stage and said, 'Ladies and gentlemen, we're sorry to announce that Matt Monroe is unable to perform tonight due to illness.' The audience started to murmur and from backstage we could hear some of them shouting out for their money back. Some started to boo. We felt we were in the middle of a war.

'But instead, for your enjoyment, ladies and gentlemen,' continued the compere, 'we present Cannon and Ball!' Suddenly we were on stage facing a very hostile crowd. I could understand their feelings. Having paid out a huge amount of money to see Matt Monroe, they were faced with an act they had only just heard of. So much for giving them time to leave or simmer down!

Bobby and I started our routine and really worked hard to get the audience on our side. Slowly but surely they started to listen, and by the end of the act we had them in the palms of our hands. We came off to tumultuous applause, feeling as high as kites. We had beaten the odds.

The manager came into the dressing room to congratulate us. He was so impressed with our performance that he told us he wasn't going to book another star for the rest of the week. Instead he said he was going to put us at the top of the bill. This was both good news and bad news. The bad news was that we wouldn't get more money, but the good news was that we would have our name outside in lights, like real stars. The money didn't matter at that moment. All that mattered was that 'Cannon and Ball' would glow for all to see.

The following evening we arrived at the club and purposely drove around the front to view the sight. There it was: 'CANNON AND BALL APPEARING TONIGHT' in huge neon lights. What a wonderful feeling it gave me! I finally felt we had arrived. The manager was there waiting for us and he showed us the way to the Number One dressing room. As we approached the door I saw that it had a star on it. We felt incredibly important.

Inside the dressing room was magnificent. There was a bar stacked with free drinks, a television, a shower en suite, huge easy chairs and a telephone. It was nicer than my own home. The manager told us that if we needed anything at all – the bar to be restocked, or some food – we should just ring and it would be done. He left and Bobby and I were like kids in a sweet shop. I sprawled in an easy chair while Bobby poured us two drinks. If this was how stars lived, then I wanted to be one. Preferably as soon as possible.

Showtime arrived, the music started and we made our entrance. It's a fact of life in show biz that it's often difficult for comedians to build up the essential relationship with an audience when the stage lights are too bright. You honestly can't see anything but a huge, white glare and an even bigger black hole. Building that relationship with the audience is vital to success, however, so we always tried our best to see who was 'out there'. We bounded out into the blackness and I immediately noticed a guy called Freddy Starr sitting at one of the front tables. Freddy is one of the funniest guys in show biz – he's the type of comic no performer wants to follow because he's too funny. Now he was watching us, and as we were working I kept taking sneaky looks at him. To my relief I saw that he was laughing along with everyone else. It made me very proud to think that this great comic found us funny. Later Freddy came to see us. He told us that we were good and he wouldn't mind us being on his show sometime. It felt good to be in the presence of such a funny man.

The following night we turned up early at the club because we wanted to spend some time in the star dressing room, and we also wanted another glimpse of our neon sign as we drove past. As we pulled up outside the club I honestly thought I was dreaming, for there in front of us was a huge sign saying 'FREDDY STARR TONIGHT'. I don't think I have ever been so dumbstruck in my life.

My heart sank. I looked at Bobby and there was no need for him to say anything because I could see it in his eyes. We went into the club and found that we were no longer in the star dressing room, but had been put back in the support acts' room. As we were still trying to work out what had happened, Freddy put his head round our door and said, 'Hello lads!' We just nodded as he closed the door and left. It was obvious that he didn't know the manager had promised us we could top the bill all week.

We didn't say anything about the change and the manager dodged us all week. We tried to pretend that everything was all right, but inside I was destroyed. It had been my one night of topping a bill properly and I had enjoyed it immensely. Not only that, but we had proved that Cannon and Ball could take the top position, not just by accident but because we honestly deserved it.

We returned to the Fiesta several times after that, and on one occasion they asked us to do a very strange thing. The new manager had this idea of putting a pantomime on in the afternoon and going back to being a cabaret club in the evening. He offered us double money, and the opportunity to try our hand in this classic theatrical art was tempting, so we agreed.

The day arrived to do the pantomime and the manager explained his ingenious method of presenting the many scenes needed for such a production. The scenery was painted onto a huge book and two 'dolly birds' would turn each page every time a new scene was required. The cast was made up of different acts who were appearing at the club that week. The drummer, a guy called Terry Clayton, played the Dame. He was an overexuberant guy who never did things by half. The manager opted out of any proper direction for his cast and basically left us to our own devices. As none of us had done a pantomime before, it was likely to turn into a circus, and it did.

We decided to put a 'slosh routine' in, when we would hit each other in the face with custard pies. Although we had seen plenty of pantos we had never actually performed in one, so we had to guess how to make the 'custard' slosh. Somebody suggested that it was made with flour and water, so we set about our preparations. Our culinary ignorance meant we didn't realize that such a mixture would become quite hard after it had sat around for a while waiting to be used.

The afternoon came and we started to perform the pantomime. It was going quite well until we came to the slosh scene. Terry, playing the Dame, was supposed to hit me in the face with the custard pie. He ran across the stage, and BAM! He'd hit me in the face with the slosh, which by this time had gone almost rock hard. I felt as if a 10-ton truck had hit me! Surely something about that wasn't right. We carried on, and I started to feel something trickling from my nose. Reaching up, I found that blood was running down my face. When we came off Terry was very apologetic.

'Look, Terry,' I said, wiping more blood from my nose, 'you're hitting me too hard. You've just got to pretend. Just pretend you're going to hit me, and when you're a couple of inches from my face just touch me with it.'

'Oh right, Tommy,' he said, 'I'll get it right tomorrow.'

'No,' I insisted, 'we'll get it right now. Let's practise.'

We practised and finally he got it, running at me as if to smash me hard in the face with the custard pie, but in the end just touching me with it.

Next day found us repeating our extravaganza. When we came to the slosh routine Terry ran across the stage, and once again, BAM! He'd hit me full in the face. The blood started pouring down from my nose even worse than before. I couldn't do anything about it on stage, and after recovering my swimming head I carried on wiping away the blood and hoped it wouldn't be noticed by the audience.

As soon as I came off I stormed into Terry's dressing room. 'What the hell are you doing?' I shouted at him.

'Sorry, Tommy,' he replied, looking sorrowful. 'I forgot!'

'You forgot!' I shouted. 'You forgot! Your forgetting is getting me a broken nose!'

'It won't happen again, Tommy,' he promised.

'You're bl**dy right it won't happen again!' I answered. 'Because if you don't get it right tomorrow there'll be trouble.' I slammed the door behind me and got outside, only to trip over Bobby, who was bowed over with laughter. 'And that goes for you too,' I growled at him as I passed, but it was to no avail. Bobby's giggling increased as I walked away.

The next day came and we reached the slosh routine. Terry looked at me and I looked at him. He ran across the stage. BAM! He'd done it again. He'd made my nose bleed and I felt as if I was in a boxing ring. This time there was no holding me back. The anger was rising right up from my feet. I started out across the stage to get him. He let out a scream and ran off the stage with me in hot pursuit. I don't know what the audience thought, but at that moment I didn't care. Terry ran into his dressing room and locked the door.

'Come out!' I screamed. 'I'm going to kill you!'

'Somebody get the police!' Terry shouted from inside his dressing room. 'He's lost it! He's crazy!'

I hammered on his door, screaming obscenities, for what seemed an age. Then I calmed down and went into my own dressing room to rest my throbbing nose. I heard the music playing and knew that the pantomime was finished when Bobby came into my room.

'All right, snozzle,' he said. 'Have you battered him then?'

'No,' I replied. 'He wouldn't come out of his room.' By this time I had calmed down and was feeling a little ashamed for frightening Terry as I had done. 'Go and see if Terry's all right for me, Bobby,' I said.

Bobby left and within two minutes he was back. 'He won't come out,' Bobby said between bouts of laughter. 'He says you've gone crackers and that you're going to kill him!'

I went to Terry's room myself, and sure enough the

door was still locked. 'Terry?' I said, knocking gently on his door. 'Terry?'

'Leave me alone,' Terry answered. 'I'm not coming out! You'll kill me!'

After about an hour of coaxing I finally got him to open the door. When he saw that I had calmed down he couldn't stop apologizing. I told him not to worry. We wouldn't be doing the slosh routine any more, so there would be no chance of me getting a broken nose. We did the rest of the pantomime performances minus the slosh routine, and ever since then I have dreaded slosh routines in any panto we have ever done.

The clubs were always full of odd characters. Some were nice and others most certainly were not. The Seven Sisters was a pub in Walthamstow, London, and was an unusual booking for us to take because we had stopped doing pubs by this time. I suppose this was different because it was a big venue which booked acts for the whole week. It had a large cabaret room and a good house band, and we looked forward to doing it, even though the place had a dubious reputation.

We arrived at the club to be met as usual by the manager, who made us very welcome. The welcoming of an act by the manager is a little bit of a show business tradition, and of course he wants to make sure that his 'vehicle' for making money is as comfortable as possible. Luckily this manager was from somewhere up north himself, so he took us under his wing. We opened the first night and did really well, getting good laughs – enough for the manager to buy us a drink (which was unusual, believe me).

The next night we did well again and later in the evening a band called The Rubettes came in. They were a group who had some hit records in the seventies and we really enjoyed their music, ending up having a jam with them on stage. Bobby was in his element. I think he always yearned to be a rock singer, but you don't find many five-foot four-inch rock stars.

When we went on stage on the third night I noticed a table of about six guys at the back of the room. They had no women with them and they didn't laugh. In fact, they didn't even smile – except for one man, who laughed all the way through. This is very off-putting for a comedian, and you end up focusing on the ones who aren't laughing, doing your best to force them into the swing of things.

I thought this party was particularly strange because they didn't have ladies with them, and the guy who was laughing was wearing a hat. He never took it off and it was pretty hot in that room. No matter, all went well and although we couldn't get the odd guys to laugh, the act finished to great cheers and applause as usual.

As was our custom, we came out of the dressing room and headed straight for the bar. Like most performers directly after a gig, we were on a high. We'd done our job and now it was time to enjoy ourselves. The two pints we ordered tasted really good. As we were savouring the moment, the manager suddenly appeared and told us that the guy in the hat had invited us over for a drink. I looked across and the man was beckoning us over to his table. I nudged Bobby and he watched as the guy waved us over once more. It got us both annoyed because it was less a wave than a command. Before I could stop Bobby, he put two fingers up at him. The manager's eyes widened, and quick as a flash he put himself between us and the guy in the hat.

'What are you doing?' he hissed.

'He's not beckoning us over as though we're his servants!' Bobby answered indignantly.

'Bobby's right,' I said, sticking up for my friend. 'I mean, if he wants to buy us a drink he should come over here, not wave us over to him as if we're two dogs.'

The manager couldn't believe what he was hearing. 'Do you know who that is?' he said, looking at us both intently.

'No,' I replied, 'we haven't got a clue.'

'It's just somebody in a hat,' Bobby chipped in, 'and if you don't mind me saying, he looks stupid.'

The manager was becoming more irate by the second. 'It's Jack the Hat!' he said finally, his voice lowering to a whisper.

'Well, that doesn't mean anything to me,' I replied. 'I just think he's very ignorant treating us like this.'

'Look, trust me, just go over to his table,' the manager said, resigning himself to the fact that we hadn't the faintest idea who he was talking about. 'Even if you don't have a drink, just say hello to the guy.'

'OK, but only as a favour to you,' I said, and dragged Bobby over to the table.

When we reached Jack the Hat, he put his hand out to greet us. He looked a strange character with his hat on, but seemed very amenable. He nodded at two of the guys sitting with him and they got up, leaving two empty chairs facing him.

'Good show that, boys, will you join me for a drink?' he asked, motioning us to sit down.

'No, thank you – we have two drinks at the bar,' I replied, not wanting to hurt his feelings.

'OK,' he said, 'I'll be in tomorrow and then will you have a drink with me?'

'No problems,' Bobby said from behind me, obviously taking a sudden liking to the guy. 'Oh, and I'm sorry about putting two fingers up at you,' he said as an afterthought.

Jack the Hat threw his head back and laughed. 'That's OK,' he said. 'I've had that all my life.'

We went back to the bar and asked the manager exactly who they were. 'Let's just say they're guys you don't mess with,' he told us. We shrugged our shoulders, returned to our drinks and, as was becoming customary, ended up getting drunk together.

When we started the run the manager had warned us that when it came to Thursday we shouldn't be too bothered about what we did because the audience would be really bad. He said it would be a mixture of men and women and all they would want to do was get drunk and get off with each other. The main entertainment of the night would be throwing beer mats at the acts. He suggested that when Thursday came we should just do as long as we could stand and then get off the stage.

The next night was the dreaded Thursday. We went into the club and I sneaked a peek around the curtains. This was something I'd always done – and still do to this day. I think it's my way of trying to assess whether we're in for a good night or a bad one. As I stared out at the rabble that night I knew this was going to be a bad one. They were already loud and on the way to being totally plastered, at least an hour before we were even due on stage. I told Bobby and he went white. It's all right for a comic to die on stage, but to be told the night before doesn't help. We'd been worried all day. We agreed that if they started throwing anything we would exit fast.

Born with a cheeky face – Bobby at Infant School (front row extreme left).

Tommy in the early days.

The 'Sherrel Brothers'' first publicity shot. Dig those haircuts!

Bobby and Yvonne on their wedding day, with the cake surrounded by beer!

Hitting the big time – Cannon and Ball in 1979.
© *London Weekend Television*

The never-ending round of a long summer season had obviously got to Tommy!

Take Two! Bobby finally met his match in singer Leo Sayer, special guest on one of their TV shows. © *BFI Films: Stills, Posters and Designs*

Surely they could have afforded to see a dentist by now! © *London Weekend Television*

The name of 'Cannon and Ball' on the poster alone was enough to draw the crowds.

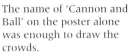

The Boys in Blue.
© The Ronald Grant Archive

A magician and his assistant. Eat your heart out, Paul Daniels!
© Topham Picturepoint

I thought there was only one Father Christmas? © *The Ronald Grant Archive*

An old bazaar in Cairo, with Kenny Lynch looking worried.
© *The Ronald Grant Archive*

Rock 'n' rollers meet onstage with Cliff Richard. © *BFI Films: Stills, Posters and Designs*

'Run, Rabbit, Run', with Tommy looking as if he is about to produce a shot gun! © *London Weekend Television*

Tommy and family.

A song and dance routine on the tribute show for friend Eric Morecambe.
© *Pearson Television*

Tommy got the 'hole in one' but Bobby can't believe it. With fellow golfer Jimmy Tarbuck. © *BFI Films: Stills, Posters and Designs*

The Tax Man
Cometh?
© *Topham Picturepoint*

Babes in the Wood.
They never really
grew up!
© *Topham Picturepoint*

It came to our turn to go on and as our opening music played we bounded on stage expecting to be booed off immediately, but the response we received was the total opposite. We were astonished. We started the act and I noticed that the guys who had been sitting at Jack the Hat's table the evening before were now standing in different positions all around the room. Jack sat on his own at the table, laughing ostentatiously at our jokes. It was obvious that somehow he had warned everybody beforehand. The audience were well behaved, almost polite, and although they didn't receive us as well as the crowd had on the other nights, at least there were no beer mats thrown. We did our full 40 minutes.

Afterwards we joined Jack at his table and he made us feel really welcome. 'I'm going to a party in the West End,' he said. 'Do you want to come?'

'No thanks, we're going to a party back at the hotel,' I lied. Bobby and I had seen the sort of power this guy had, and a few worrying thoughts were beginning to click into place.

'OK,' he said, 'no problems. We'll see you at the weekend.'

We never did see him again. A few months later we heard that the Kray Twins had been arrested in connection with the murder of a guy named Jack the Hat. When we saw his photograph in the paper we couldn't believe our eyes. It was the same Jack we had met in the Seven Sisters pub. We shuddered to think what might have happened if we had accepted his sinister invitation to that West End party.

CHAPTER EIGHT

STRIPPERS AND BOUNCERS

A life on the club circuit had a culture and community all of its own in the early eighties. Spending so long travelling from one town to the next each day creates the possibility of becoming totally separate from the reality of normal, everyday existence. This 'unplugged' sensation arises from the daily round of rising mid-morning; clambering into the car for the long trek to the next club, which could easily be several hundred miles away; arriving late afternoon to unpack at the digs; setting off to the club to prepare for the performance; doing the gig; drinking at the bar; and finally arriving back at the bed and breakfast at anything up to four o'clock in the morning – only to repeat the whole process the next day. This treadmill goes on seven days a week and is accompanied by constant emotional upheaval. The buzz of an appreciative audience can lead to arrogant pride engendered by adoring fans, and gives way to the slow slide into a trough of despair as the effects of the after-show drinks take hold. It isn't long before one day becomes very much like another. With the extensive travelling they undertook at this time, Bobby seriously felt he could easily pass a degree in geography.

The thing that amused me about our journeys was the names that some of these venues had. Despite being located in a seedy back street of Manchester, they would still proudly display titles such as The Ocean 11 Club, The Club Del Sol, Mr Smith's, Fagin's. These were the popular places where people could be entertained from the mid-seventies.

The clubs would be open all week, but usually Wednesdays and Thursdays were stag nights. The rest of the week would be family entertainment. A stag night consisted of a comic and a stripper doing alternate spots until the night was over. It was certainly a mind-blowing thing for Tommy and me at first. The first time we did such a show I thought I was the luckiest man alive. We got our first booking and set out anticipating a night of excitement in the company of strippers where hopefully all our fantasies would come true. How quickly we found out that it would be business as usual!

We arrived at the club and went into the dressing room, and there were about six models in various stages of undress. I had never seen so many naked women at the same time before, and hey, I was getting paid to do this job! I thought it was my birthday and gave the girls my sexiest smile. Tommy and I were soon disappointed when we found that the strippers were far too busy drinking cups of tea and smoking even to notice us.

Our turn came to go on stage and the stripper who had preceded us stalked off and threw her feather boa into the room. She was a beautiful-looking lady with a face like Grace Kelly and the body of Pamela Anderson. 'Bleedin' animals!' she shouted. 'They want me to go on again, but I can't because I have to take the bloody kids to school tomorrow!'

I stood there open mouthed. This beautiful creature, who moments earlier had been on stage exuding eroticism and sexual excitement, was now screaming her head off like a fishwife. It just didn't seem to fit. I soon learned that it was just a job to the girls, nothing more and nothing less. They got paid for showing their bodies and that's all there was to it. Away from the clubs they lived ordinary lives with the same problems everybody else had.

To be a comic in a stag show you had to resort to blue gags and hard swearing. I realize this is the norm for many young comics today, and I think that something has been lost because of this, but in our younger days you couldn't swear or tell really blue gags to a family audience. For the stag shows, however, where the audience was men only, it was not only expected but demanded.

This worried us then, as it still does today. Even though it may seem like old-fashioned values, I still believe that a comedian doesn't have to resort to swearing and blue gags in order to be funny. It's *harder* to be funny being clean. We tried to be blue doing the stag shows, with Tommy telling me to f*** off and me returning his comment with a similar curse, but it didn't work for us. We even felt dirty and almost as if we were cheating our audience – we weren't giving them what we did best. So we started being ultra-clean at those stag shows. The strange thing was that it worked, probably because the audience would eventually get tired of see-ing strippers and hearing blue comedians. We became a refreshing change for them and they appreciated us for being clean. I think we eventually became the only clean act on the stag circuit in Manchester.

One week we got a series of bookings right up in the Northeast. Those seven days were to change my life. With the painful memories of my marriage break-up still at the back of my mind, I was certainly not looking for another relationship. I'm not saying I was Mr Goody-Goody – I would certainly have made the most of any lonely stripper coming my way – but I just didn't want to be tied down. Tommy was no saint either, and with his own marriage heading for the rocks, he began to wine and dine the ladies. In later years he had a girl-friend in every port and as we toured the country he would look them up whenever he was in their area. By contrast, I wasn't interested in having a girlfriend and I would certainly have been horrified at the thought of marriage!

Tommy and I had been invited to an after-show party by another act touring with us, and when we got there it was in full swing. We soon got into the party mood, helped by a few bottles of Newcastle Brown. I was sitting in an old armchair sipping my beer, when in walked the loveliest creature I had ever seen. The miniskirt, leather boots and fur coat were all that a man could dream of. I desperately wanted to say hello, but she was with another man and I knew I had to wait for my opportunity.

Yvonne was a tall girl, and as I watched her for the rest of the evening, doubts about ever being able to attract her increased steadily within me. She had lovely long legs and I had such short ones. What chance did I have? The party was soon over and we all stumbled back to our digs. Amazingly enough, it was just two days later at another party that I saw this fascinating woman once more, and this time I was determined to speak to her.

I felt a little rush of excitement run through me and I wondered to myself how I could get to speak to her and make an impression. I realized from her demeanour and how she dressed that she was a bit of a rebel, so she obviously wouldn't like to be given orders. That was it! That was going to be my plan. She was just in front of me, so I stood up and tapped her on the shoulder.

'Listen,' I said, 'I'm going to the toilet and when I get back I hope you aren't sat in my chair.' Then I left. Yvonne told me later that this really annoyed her and she thought, 'How could such a little man talk to me like that?' It obviously worked, however, because when I got back she was sitting in my chair just as I had anticipated.

'Could I have my chair back?' I asked.

She got out of the chair and I sat down. I could see that she had never been spoken to like this before and it obviously fascinated her. She asked me my name and where I came from, and before I knew where I was she was kneeling in front of me and we were talking as if we had known each other all our lives. I felt so at ease with her. After all the pain of my first marriage it felt good to be so comfortable with another woman. Even though Yvonne had incredible legs and a great body, it was her eyes that attracted me the most. She had the most wondrous eyes I have ever seen on anyone. They were brown but sad, and I wanted to take her in my arms and tell her that everything was going to be all right.

She told me that she was a waitress at a local nightclub and that I was welcome to go and see her there any time I wanted. That night we talked about every subject under the sun and before we knew it, the sun was coming up. We had stayed up all night talking. When I asked if I could see her the following night she agreed. I met her at the nightclub where she worked, and continued to see her night after night.

It soon became time for me to go back to Oldham, and I found that I was in love with Yvonne. We wanted to keep seeing each other, so I would travel 100 miles from Oldham to Stockton-on-Tees three times a week. It didn't matter. Just seeing Yvonne was all that mattered. Eventually we decided to get married, and it was the best decision of my life. I knew in my heart that she was my soulmate, and I knew deep down that we would stay together.

Romance was one thing, success in the business was another, however. Although I now had Yvonne by my side, it didn't stop me taking advantage pretty early on in our relationship. The long days away from home continued, and to keep myself from boredom there wasn't much that I was afraid to get involved with, when it was offered.

We were very busy at this time, travelling from venue to venue. Much of it merged into a blur of very similar experiences, but some occasions still stand out in my memory. After a prestigious gig at the Ace of Clubs in Leeds one night, Tommy and I were feeling a little excitable. It was a 'double night' of gigs and as we entered the second club by the back door I saw a guy standing there with his back to me. He was wearing a top hat, a tailcoat and white gloves, and was holding a cane. I could see that he was waiting to be announced to go on stage. Being the friendly person that I am, I came up behind him and slapped him on the back, saying, 'How are you, mate!'

I knew something was wrong because he just stood there and looked at me as if he wanted to kill me. I was wondering what I could have done that was so wrong when I noticed a feather float down from underneath his coat. It suddenly dawned on me that he was a magician. When I knocked him on the back I hit one of the doves secreted inside his coat. I don't think I killed it, but I must have given the poor bird a bad headache, because when he went on to do his act the dove wouldn't come out. The magician didn't speak to Tommy and me for the rest of the week, even though I apologized. It only widened the gap of appreciation that magicians and I already had for one another!

Apart from such little mishaps our reputation as a good act increased steadily, and this started to open new doors for us. One was an offer to work abroad. Australia and South Africa beckoned. Neither Tommy nor I had been abroad before, and for two ex-welders sitting on Bondi Beach it felt as if God was really smiling down on us. We had some great times whilst we were abroad, but as usual there were also some very hairy moments.

It was in South Africa that I nearly became a pimp. We were working there for six weeks, but by the end of the fourth week Tommy and I were getting short of money. We were desperate, in fact. We were in the bar of the hotel where we were working when in walked an old Jewish woman. I recognized her because she had been at our show the previous night and it was obvious that she found Tommy attractive. She was about 76 years old and dripping in gold, so she wasn't short of a pound or two. As I watched her chat to Tommy, a little plan formed in my head. When she eventually went off to buy herself a drink, I began to share my cunning plan.

'Listen Tommy,' I said, 'I know how we can get some money.'

'How?' he asked, his eyes lighting up.

'See that lady over there?' I continued. 'She's obviously got the hots for you, so why don't you chat her up and maybe she'll give you some money.'

He slowly swivelled around on his bar stool and surveyed the room. Then he swivelled back to me and said, 'There's nobody in the bar except the old lady in the corner.'

'She's the one I mean,' I said, trying to raise some enthusiasm. 'Just chat her up a bit more, and tell her you spotted her last night and that you fancy her.'

He looked at me as if I had lost my mind. Then he looked over once again to the lady. 'Are you crazy?' he said, his voice dropping to a whisper. 'She's old enough to be my grandmother!'

'Look, Tommy,' I said, putting an arm around his shoulder. 'We have no money, right?'

'Right,' he answered.

'Well, look at her – she's got gold coming out of her ears! All you have to do is go over there, buy her a drink, mention that we're a bit short of cash, and Bob's your uncle.'

I could see that Tommy was thinking it through and slowly coming around to my plan. 'I'm not sleeping with her,' he eventually said, with determination in his voice.

'No! You don't have to sleep with her! Unless it's necessary,' I quipped as an afterthought.

'Forget it!' Tommy shouted.

'Keep your voice down!' I hissed at him. 'Just go over there and see what happens.' It was beginning to look like a scene from the film *Midnight Cowboy* with John Voight and Dustin Hoffman.

'OK,' Tommy said eventually. 'But you'll owe me for this.'

I patted him on the back and he started to walk over to the old lady. Her eyes lit up as she saw him coming across the room towards her. When Tommy was halfway across the room, however, he turned and walked back to me.

'I can't do it!' he said putting his head in his hands. 'I'd sooner starve. Sorry Bobby.'

I took another look at the woman and realized that I had nearly become a pimp. 'I was only joking,' I said, hoping that he would believe me.

'You weren't,' he replied. 'You would have had me sleeping with her for money.'

'No Tommy,' I said, trying to make light of the situation. 'She's far too young for you!' He laughed and we went on with our drinking. Since then, when people ask what I did before I was a comic, Tommy always says, 'He was a pimp.'

Summer seasons were obviously the next step up from the nightclub circuit, and we were delighted when we were offered our first one in Guernsey. Being able to stay in one place for some time was a welcome change. On the bill were four dancers, a magician called Bunny Nield, a vocal trio called The Song Spinners and, at the top of the bill, a tenor called Kevin Ross. It was a good bill for a small resort and it was during this summer season that Tommy and I changed our characters once more, thanks to a singer called Harry.

At that time Tommy and I wore mohair suits and looked like two Jimmy Tarbucks on stage. It wasn't very original. I'm not saying that Jimmy isn't original. He's by far one of the best stand-up comedians we have in this country. It's just that there were plenty of double acts in those days like Tommy and me and we needed to be more different. It took someone else to help us see this, however.

Harry, the lead singer of The Song Spinners, came to us one day and said, 'You need to look at your act, lads.'

'Why?' we asked defensively, thinking he was going to say we were no good.

'The act is good as it is,' he said, 'but you're like loads of other double acts. You need to be different.'

'How?' I asked, getting interested in what he had to say.

'Well,' he continued, 'if Bobby got a funny suit and Tommy picked on him, then you'd have the basis to develop a better and more original double act. People could also identify with your characters. Do you know what I mean?'

We did. That night Tommy and I missed the usual round of drinks and went straight back to our digs for a serious discussion. We stayed up nearly all night talking it through. Knowing Harry was right in what he was saying, we still found it difficult to work out how to make the change. The discussion filled our dreams that night, and we continued it the next morning and into the following weeks.

Back in 'clubland' after the summer season, we eventually decided that the act would consist of Tommy being the 'star', while I played a character whose one aim in life was to get Tommy's autograph and become his friend. This character would desperately want to be liked and would even dress like his hero if possible. My body language would need to be like that of a small boy, and I would demand the audience's sympathy whilst Tommy bullied me.

The next step was to find the costumes to give us this image. We wrote 20 minutes of material to see if the idea would work and then went into town to buy some clothes. Tommy's were easy – he just needed the smartest suit we could find. For 'little Bobby' it was much harder, and even though we wandered round all the shops we couldn't find anything that matched my new character. After searching for a couple of hours we were on the verge of giving up when we strolled past an Oxfam shop. There in the window was the ideal thing – a dress suit that would have fitted a 20-stone man. It was huge, but perfect for what I wanted. I bought it for less than a pound.

Next door was a shoe shop and a pair of light brown Hush Puppies caught my eye. These were obviously the worst shoes to match the black suit, and they were just what I needed. When we got back to our digs I tried the costume on. It was gigantic, it looked perfect, and most of all I suddenly felt funny. Out of necessity I added a pair of red braces, as the trousers were way too big for me. Little did I know that these braces would become my trademark in later years.

Tommy and I rehearsed our new act and the night soon came when we were going to try it out for the first time. We decided that when Tommy was introduced on stage, the characters' image would be enhanced if I was to enter from the audience. I would ask for Tommy's autograph and he would invite me onto the stage. The act would develop from there.

It was quite an original idea for those days, but I think I may have overdone it a little. When we got to the venue that night I saw people queuing up to go in and decided to join them. That way, I surmised, people would really think that I was part of the audience. I stood in line and started to tell the people nearest me how much I liked Tommy Cannon, saying he was my hero and generally making a nuisance of myself. I don't know what they thought about this little guy in an oversized suit gabbling on about Tommy Cannon, but it was too late to turn back now, so I did it even more.

We went into the cabaret room and I sat at a table with some other people and noticed some strange looks as I took my character overboard. I enjoyed the early parts of the show and wondered if anyone had missed me at all backstage. Before long Tommy was announced and went straight into a song. I jumped up and started to shout across the tables at him. 'Tommy! Tommy!' I shouted. 'Can I have your autograph?'

The other people on my table glared at me and told me to sit down, but soon discovered I wasn't taking any notice of them. We did the act just the way we had rehearsed, and as soon as people realized that I was part of the act and not just a drunk from the audience they loved it. This was the start of a new beginning for Cannon and Ball. We had found originality.

They say the best comedy is discovered not created, and I found that whilst I was on stage my braces kept sliding off my shoulders, like some bra straps do, I suppose (not that I know much about that!). The more they slipped off, the more I pulled them up and the more the audience laughed. I started to exaggerate the whole thing and it got howls of laughter in return, so we kept it in.

The catchphrase happened by accident too. David Essex had just released 'Rock On', his new single. It was a great song and everyone was singing it, including me. When Tommy came on stage one night, I shouted, 'Rock on, Tommy!' and repeated it whenever I had the chance. Before long everybody was saying it to us! We would just be walking down the street and people would shout out, 'Rock on, Tommy!' Later we even sold braces with 'Rock on, Tommy!' written on them.

Our year now consisted of a summer season, then clubs and pantomime in the winter. One of the first pantos we did was at the Liverpool Empire with a lady for whom both Tommy and I have great respect – Cilla Black. As principal boy she looked great in those thigh-slapping tights, and one night she got a marvellous laugh that proved to be a very unique one-off.

Awaiting our entrance, we stood in the wings watching her perform. It was the part in the panto where she had to fight the baddie. As she tussled with him, all the kids were yelling out for Cilla to win in true pantomime fashion. She finally beat the baddie and pinned him to the floor, looming over him with her sword. The kids cheered and then went quiet as they wondered what Cilla would do with the trembling victim. She looked straight at the audience and said, 'How shall I punish him, kids?'

As quick as a flash, one kid shouted back in a broad Liverpool accent, 'Sing to him, Cilla!' The audience went wild. It got the biggest laugh of the season. Cilla broke down laughing and it took her at least five minutes to get her self-composure back.

From the outside, show business seems to be a glamorous career, but sometimes things aren't so nice on the inside. Tommy and I were beginning to get very popular when we got a booking to perform at The Troubadour club in Cardiff. By that time we had employed a personal assistant. He would drive us to gigs and generally look after us. Phil Noden was a lovely man and very good at the difficult job of running around after a couple of comics like us. He was also a karate expert and used to do unarmed combat training for the police. He was a useful man to have in your corner in case of any trouble.

We did the first night at The Troubadour and got a call from the club the following morning, asking us if we could come over immediately. This was very strange because clubs are normally well closed at that time of day.

For the management of the club to phone us so early, something had to be seriously wrong. We got to the club to find two CID policemen waiting for us. They asked us to go into the club's office because there was something they wanted us to listen to. They played us a tape, and what I heard made my skin crawl. Somebody had left a message on the club's answering machine about us, and I can only describe their voice as evil. This person apparently felt nothing but pure hate for Tommy and me.

The terrifying voice on the tape said, 'I hate Cannon and Ball and I'm going to kill them. They don't know what they do to me and it's payback time. I'm going to kill Tommy Cannon first and then take my time with Bobby Ball. I shall enjoy ripping his moustache out hair by hair. He'll wish that he was dead by the time I've finished with him.'

This sent shivers down my spine, and it frightened me to think that somebody could hate us that much without us knowing why. The police took it very seriously and said we had to be guarded the whole week we were appearing in Cardiff. They assigned two officers to pick us up from our hotel at night and stay with us until we were back. Every evening they would wait to take us to the club and after our show would bundle us into a waiting police car, driving us straight back to the hotel. I felt as if I was in some kind of hostage situation. Being well known was one thing, but if this was what prime ministers and other high-profile figures had to put up with, they could keep it!

The first night after hearing the message we went on stage with our hearts in our mouths. At any moment we expected to hear a shot ring out and one of us to fall down dead. It certainly took the edge off the act that week. After about three nights of this, however, the police dropped us back at the hotel and left. We presumed they must think the danger was over.

At reception, the night porter said that another policeman had been in asking for us. Phil, our PA, asked whether the officer had left a name. Yes, said the porter, he said he was PC Green. Had he seen a gun or any other weapon on the man? The night porter said he couldn't be sure, but the man looked to have a bulge underneath his coat. Phil called the police station to check if an Officer Green had been to the hotel that night. It turned out that there wasn't an Officer Green stationed in Cardiff. This caused much concern. The police rushed back to the hotel and took a statement from the night porter.

By this time it was about three o'clock in the morning and I was getting really tired – not that I could have slept, mind you! Nonetheless, I told Phil I was going to try and get some sleep and he said he would check out my room first. I told him not to bother, I would be all right, but he insisted on making it look like something out of a James Bond movie. He returned with the 'all clear' and left me to flop into bed. I felt safe because Phil and the police were downstairs and they had said they would stay on duty all night.

Imagine my surprise in the morning, when I had dressed and opened my door to go downstairs for breakfast – there was Phil, fast asleep in the corridor across my doorway. I laughed and laughed. He didn't wake up, so I stepped over him and went down to breakfast. About 10 minutes later he came running into the restaurant in a panic.

'What's the matter, Phil?' I asked him, with the picture of him sleeping in the corridor still in my mind.

'Thank goodness you're here,' he said, gasping. 'I thought you'd been kidnapped!'

This only made me splutter and cough over my orange juice. I think it was one of the best laughs we had on that tour. Phil couldn't believe that I was taking a death threat so lightly, but I believed that if the guy had been seriously intending to do any damage, he would have done it by then. Nothing happened to us, and in fact they soon caught the guy, but we made many friends in the Cardiff police force and Phil proved how invaluable he was.

We could have done with Phil's help not long afterwards, when we were rebooked to appear at Batley's for a week and decided to open the show with my usual appearance from the back of the auditorium. After the first night, I was having a drink with the bouncers when I had an idea for making the act look more authentic.

'Tomorrow,' I said to the biggest bruiser, 'I'll need your help.'

'Of course, Bobby,' he replied. 'What do you want me to do?'

'Well,' I continued, 'when I start to walk from the back of the room to get Tommy's autograph, wait until I'm at the front of the stage and then come and get me and pretend to throw me out.'

'Do you really want me to throw you out?' he asked.

I looked at him and realized that there probably wasn't much of a light on upstairs, but I had gone too far to turn back. 'No, just pretend,' I said. 'Then Tommy will stop you and you can let me go.'

'Oh right,' he answered, but I knew he was having difficulty understanding what I had asked.

When we got into the car, Tommy whistled between his teeth. 'Boy, you've made a mistake there!' he said.

'It'll be all right,' I answered, trying to sound as cheerful as ever.

When the following night came I went round to the back of the room and waited for Tommy to appear on stage. When he did I set off from the back, shouting at him in the usual way, 'Tommy! Tommy! Could I have your autograph?'

It was going well and I felt the audience believed it. I was in front of the stage when suddenly a hand grabbed hold of my shoulder. I turned around and there was the bouncer. 'Come on, son,' he said, obviously enjoying this tremendously, 'let's be having you out.'

'No sir, it's all right,' Tommy said from his position on stage, 'he only wants my autograph.'

'OK then,' the bouncer replied and let me go, but not before smiling directly into the spotlight. The audience saw his pose, applauded him, and he was clearly hooked. He thought he was a star.

Tommy and I did the rest of our act and we were both pleased with the opening, provided the bouncer could keep it as short as he had done that time. The following night I came from the back of the room shouting for Tommy's autograph, but this time the bouncer waited until I had climbed two steps up towards the stage.

'Come on, son,' he said, looking not at me but at the audience, 'let's be having you.'

'No, it's OK sir,' Tommy said, as he had the previous night. 'He just wants my autograph.'

But this time the bouncer didn't want to go. This was his claim to fame and he wasn't letting it slip away that easily. 'Don't worry about it, Tommy,' the bouncer continued, as he dragged me across the front of the stage towards the door. 'Just say the word and I'll have him out.'

'You're ruining the act!' I kept trying to whisper, but he was in full flow.

'We don't allow this sort of behaviour in this club, Tommy,' he went on.

'Look, he's OK, I'll sign his autograph and then he'll leave – won't you?' Tommy said, looking at me with panic in his eyes.

'Yes! Yes!' I said, staring at the bouncer and trying to signal him to let me go.

'OK then,' he said finally, dragging me back. 'Any trouble, Tommy, give me a shout.' Off he went, waving to the crowd as he made his way slowly towards the back of the club.

The following night we decided not to risk it any further. It had nearly brought the act to a standstill the night before, just as we needed to grab our audience and get the first laughs going. I went round to the front of the club to find our friend and tell him that it was all off. I searched everywhere, but to no avail. 'I couldn't find him,' I reported to Tommy. 'Maybe he's off tonight, so let's just do it as normal.'

'OK,' Tommy agreed. 'Thank goodness there won't be any bouncer to mess it up this time.'

Just before our entrance I went to the back of the room and finding that the bouncer was still nowhere to be seen, I started to relax. Tommy came on stage, started

137

to sing, and I went forward as usual. I was about three foot from the stage when the missing bouncer jumped up from behind a table and wrestled me to the ground. Tommy jumped off the stage and tried to get the guy off me. 'Don't worry, Tommy!' he shouted, with one eye on the spotlight. 'I've got him!'

We wrestled our way onto the stage and now the bouncer was really in his element. This was the first time he had actually been on the stage. He let go of me and we all stood there for a moment trying to get our breath back.

'I've told you before about trying to upset Mr Cannon,' the bouncer said, pointing a finger at me. Tommy and I looked at each other. Had he gone totally mad?

'Well, thank you,' Tommy said calmly, 'I'll take it from here.'

'OK Tommy,' the bouncer replied. 'Any trouble, just give me a shout.'

The audience just stared at us open mouthed. We didn't know if we could get them back or not after the fiasco that had just unfolded before their eyes, but we did our best. They were obviously confused by what had happened, but we managed some laughs, though it was obvious we hadn't gone down as well as normal. We finished the act and went back to our dressing room. When we got there the bouncer was waiting for us.

'Brilliant!' he said, as if he thought everything was all right. 'I decided to ad-lib a bit, that's why I hid behind the table so that I could catch you unawares. Good, eh? But tomorrow I think we should have a little more dialogue between us.' Was this man crazy, or what? He had just ruined our act and now he wanted a bigger part in it! I wished I had never thought of the idea.

'There won't be any more dialogue, mate,' Tommy said to him sternly. 'We're not doing it tomorrow night. We're changing the act.'

The bouncer looked heartbroken and left the dressing room in silence. Tommy and I looked at each other, expressions of enormous relief on our faces. We later heard that the bouncer told everyone we had dropped the routine because he was getting bigger laughs than we were. Maybe he was right!

In all the haze and mist of life in show biz, family life continued back at home. By now we had Joanne, our new daughter, who looked as beautiful as her mum. My focus was not on the family, however. Despite the success and the full diary, we had still not hit the big time. That was still ahead of us. Not that we hadn't been flirting with it, of course. Fame is a cruel mistress and it's easy to become addicted to her. She takes all you have and spits you out when she has no further use for you. Tommy and I were already courting Lady Fame, and we were about to find out exactly how deadly she was.

CHAPTER NINE

THE FAME GAME

Andy Warhol once predicted that we would all enjoy 15 minutes of fame at some time in our lives. Fifteen minutes is probably just as much as anybody could reasonably stand, for fame is a hugely powerful force. It can shoot you to heights of pleasure and plunge you to depths of depression never previously encountered. Its destructive nature can work unseen inside you like a cancer, while the public face continues to smile. Worst of all, fame is beyond your control. The performer is fame's puppet not its master. You are top of the charts one week and bottom the next. One minute the audience calls for more and the next they boo you off. For Bobby and Tommy the top of the ladder came soon enough, only to throw their personal lives into complete disarray. Bobby explains how before long the only sanity and stability in their lives came when they were on stage.

Humphrey Barclay, an influential producer for London Weekend Television, saw us do our first Blackpool season in 1981 and was impressed with how we handled our audience. He introduced himself to us after the show and offered us the chance to do some sketches for a new series that he was preparing, *Brucie's Big Night Out*. There was no need to audition, no 'perhaps' or 'maybe'

– this was a definite offer. We agreed the deal and Humphrey said he would make arrangements with our manager. (By this time we had two managers, one who lived near us in Oldham and one in London.) The whole scene was straight from some 'unknown shot to stardom' movie, and Tommy and I went home as high as kites. If we hadn't had a car we would have flown home on our excitement.

When the time came for us to record the sketches we were doing a summer season in Great Yarmouth, and topping the bill was a certain comedian called Larry Grayson. He was a wonderful camp comic who could hold the audience in the palm of his hand after just a turn of his head. He was also a gracious man, because he let us go to London every day to record the sketches, despite the risk of being late for the evening show. As Larry topped the bill, it was his prerogative to be able to say we couldn't do it, but he told us to grab the chance with both hands and not to worry about his show, he would cover for us if necessary. I will always remember him fondly for that.

Every morning we caught a train to London at 6.15 and went through the newly arrived scripts on the way. Having spent the day rehearsing and recording the sketches, we caught the four o'clock train back to Yarmouth for the two evening shows. We did this for six weeks and by the end we were absolutely shattered. Exhaustion was only kept at bay by the adrenaline rush of excitement.

We finished the season, thanked Larry, and waited for Brucie's show to appear on television. The *TV Times* proudly announced Bruce Forsyth's new show, 'with sketches by Cannon and Ball'. It was better than having our name in lights. Millions could now read about us, and we finally felt we were on our way. The show was due to be aired on Saturday night and I couldn't wait. I sat glued to my chair in front of the television with all my family, waiting for the show to start. This was my big moment.

Eventually the show began. I kept waiting and waiting, thinking we would be on any minute. We watched it all the way through, even to the credits at the end, and not one of our sketches was shown. I couldn't believe it. What had gone wrong? I was heartbroken, all my family were. All that work gone to waste; all that travelling Tommy and I had done down to London and back, only for our work to end up on the cutting room floor. I was devastated. I couldn't say anything to anybody and just went straight up to bed feeling very sorry for myself. I lay there not knowing whether to scream and shout or just cry.

The next day our manager phoned and told me that, although they hadn't shown it that week, they were going to show it the following week. A reprieve! At least we were going to be shown after all. The following week came and there we were again, printed boldly in the *TV Times*: 'sketches by Cannon and Ball'. But the same thing happened, and we weren't shown. Once more my emotions felt as if they were on a roller coaster. I had got so excited about our first television appearance, knowing that all my friends and family were watching, only to be brought down to earth with a bump when once again we weren't even mentioned.

I put on a brave face when friends and family kept asking me why we weren't on the programme. I couldn't answer, so I just shrugged my shoulders and muttered something about that sort of thing happening in show business. Secretly I felt rejected and humiliated, and I was fed up with being let down. Why was I told something would happen when it obviously wasn't going to? Was this going to be the story of my life?

We eventually found out that they had got the show format wrong and that the producers were desperately moving pieces of the programme around to try and make it work. It seemed that our television career was doomed from the outset. What made it worse was that it had nothing to do with us. We'd given 100 per cent of ourselves, we'd given our best, and now others were apparently denying us the opportunity to show the country what we could do. It was just so frustrating.

It became even worse as week after week we didn't get shown, but every week we were mentioned in the *TV Times*. I wondered if this would cause an adverse response with the public too. Maybe people would think that we were just not good enough to be shown, or that we hadn't turned up at the studio. It was the press who quickly picked up on the fact of our repeated non-appearances and started to ask, 'Who *are* Cannon and Ball?' Eventually some sort of bland statement was made by the TV company, but it was never properly explained.

We never did get shown on *Brucie's Big Night Out*, but as luck would have it, encouraged a good deal by our agent Laurie Mansfield, Michael Grade saw our sketches and immediately decided that we should have our own series. Mr Grade was head of London Weekend Television and perfectly able to make decisions like this. We were very wary at first, however. By then we had a track record of people breaking their promises. Was this just another bluff? So we accepted the idea with just a little pinch of salt. We would believe it when we saw the contract, and even then it didn't mean the material would ever get aired, we thought.

It was some weeks before all the different negotiations between television producers and agents came to a halt. Telephone calls on all the different aspects of the contract were flying around, but Tommy and I stayed calm. When we were invited to discuss the length of the series, the writers who would help provide the material, and the subject of money, we began to feel that it might actually come off after all. David Bell, a brilliant light entertainment producer, was hired to put the show together for us, and an idea started to become a reality.

Then I was worrying again. Would we have enough material? It was one thing performing pretty much the same thing for 40 minutes each night, but it was quite another to come up with hours of sketches that had to work almost at once. There was no time for the usual honing and testing here – we just had to do the best we could in the time available. Of course, what I was forgetting was that in television you have the luxury of scriptwriters, and we were to be blessed with the best in the business, Sid Green. Having written for many famous comics including Morecambe and Wise, his material suited us perfectly.

Once more we gave everything to the many weeks of rehearsing and recording. It seemed strange that suddenly we had come from not getting a few sketches aired to owning our own series. I always said, 'You can't plan ahead because tomorrow has a plan of its own,' and such thoughts echoed around my head in the rare moments when my mind wasn't filled with plans for the show.

The final realization that this was not a dream came when we were told that our own theme song was being written. This was a great moment – having spent our lives singing other people's material, this one was just for us. It might have been a predicament, of course, had we not liked the song when it turned up, but when the composer, Nigel Hess, played it to us on the piano, it sounded fantastic. It seemed to mirror our lives, and 'Together We'll Be OK' became our theme tune for ever more.

The series was finally 'in the can', and we waited with immense trepidation for it to come out. Then, would you believe it, just before the series was due to broadcast, all the technicians went on strike and all ITV programmes were cancelled. There was literally just a blank screen. The days leading up to the proposed airing of our new show were traumatic. Would the strike be finished by Saturday? I just couldn't allow myself even to think that all our hard work might not reach the screen *again*. For the first time in my life, I seriously considered that somebody or something was against us.

Saturday came and the screen remained blank. I didn't know where to put myself. My anger and confusion were temporarily calmed by the fact that the press got hold of it again and started to call us 'Cannon and Blackout'. It was wonderful publicity for us, but I was still reeling from the frustration of it all. When the series eventually came out, a mixture of exuberance and disbelief that our show had finally made it almost caused me to burst. I think I went to bed with a bigger headache that night than all my late-night drinking sessions put together could ever have given me.

The series proved a huge success with the public and we were now real celebrities. Everywhere I went people would shout out 'Rock on, Tommy!' and pretend to pull their invisible braces. The venues we played were heaving with people and tickets for the shows were even being sold on the black market. When we did our next season at the North Pier in Blackpool we were the only act who had to be driven by car down the half-mile to the theatre, because the crowd was so large.

As the cash started to pour into our pockets, Tommy and I began to be swept along with the craziness of it all. We didn't look after our own money any more, but left that to an accountant appointed by our manager. We didn't know exactly how much we were earning, but we did know that all we had to do was ask and we could have. Everything was happening so fast that we seemed to be living in a constant whirlwind of demands, and sometimes I don't think Tommy and I really understood what was going on around us. The treadmill of performance, travel and sleep was endless.

Our next television series had huge stars appearing alongside us as guests. Little Richard, Status Quo, Cliff Richard, Diana Dors, Engelbert Humperdinck and even Bruce Forsyth himself joined us, and every one was a pleasure to work with. We carried on with our live gigs and recorded all the television material during the day, only this time we were driven everywhere by chauffeurs who saluted us as we stepped into the shining car.

In many ways we were in greater control of our professional lives now, and could employ young comics who we thought were very talented to work with us. We were the ones who decided who did or who didn't appear with us. Comics such as Brian Conley, Lenny

Henry and Bobby Davro all went on to become stars in their own right.

We had the luxury of our own band too, a group of great musicians who were to stay with us for the rest of our careers. Our musical directors, Mike Ryal and then Rick Coates, made sure all our music was of the highest standard. Although we were comics, music and song continued to play a very important role in the act.

We even made a film during those frenzied days. *The Boys in Blue* featured two inept policemen who bumble their way through solving a robbery. It wasn't an original film but a remake of an old Will Hay movie. Nevertheless, it was great fun to make. We were finishing one scene as dusk arrived. Dressed as two SAS men, we had to run across a field leading up to a farm with cows in the background making it look authentic. A light was meant to go on in the farmhouse and we had to throw ourselves flat on the ground, whereupon I would land on a fake cow pat.

The special effects crew proudly showed me how realistic the fake cow muck was and placed it exactly on the right mark. The director shouted 'Action!' and Tommy and I obediently ran across the field, throwing ourselves flat on the ground at the given spot. I landed perfectly, right in the middle of the mess as planned. As we said our lines I looked at Tommy and noticed that he had a strange twinkle in his eye. I looked at him again and then down at the ground where I was lying. There to one side of me was the fake cow pat. I was lying in a real one. As soon as I realized what I had done, the smell and taste hit me. It seemed to take the lining off my nose, it was so strong, and now I was stuck in the middle of a field in the middle of nowhere, covered with cow's excrement. Somehow we got to the end of the take, got up as directed and ran out of camera shot.

The crew had realized what had happened and were all laughing. I would have laughed myself, but I didn't dare open my mouth for fear of swallowing any more cow muck. With the help of the crew I cleaned off and it was only then that I learned the truth. The cow pat that I thought was fake wasn't fake at all. Both piles of muck had been shovelled there by the crew for a joke. I couldn't believe it. I thought I was playing a serious scene and all the time the crew were behind the camera just waiting for me to land in the mess. I told them it was a good joke and laughed along with them, but inside I was upset – I could still smell the cow muck after two showers.

Jokes are sometimes bad for the nerves, but mine were stretched so often that I sometimes wondered if I had any left. When we were invited to appear in our first Royal Command Performance I was particularly stressed. These shows are unlike any other. The audience pays a huge amount of money which goes to charity, just for the privilege of being there. The men are dressed up in their evening suits and the women in their best frocks and jewellery, and they don't laugh unless a member of the royal family does. The act can either do well or really struggle. There doesn't seem to be much in between.

Waiting in the wings, I couldn't stop going to the loo and nor could Tommy. Before the show started there was a terrific sense of foreboding and dread of the unknown. No one knew how their performance would be received by the Queen and her family, or by the audience, and not just those in the theatre but the millions watching at home too. There was much to be gained and a whole lot more to be lost, and it was all in the balance. Three minutes on stage and the whole thing would be decided for you.

As soon as the band struck up their opening bars the tension seemed to subside, and as the show progressed things became easier. The performers coming off stage having faced the 'monster' emanated relief and happiness, and this soon filtered through to the rest of us.

Jimmy Tarbuck was the MC for our first Royal Command. It was a pleasure watching how he manipulated the audience just by pausing between gags. He is a master 'gagman', and as telling jokes was never my big talent, I appreciate someone who can. I don't hate anyone in this business, although there are some I would call undesirable. I particularly like many of the northern comics, such as Mick Millar, Johnny Casson and The Grumbleweeds, because they are the backbone of comedy. These guys know how to face a hostile crowd and break them down. In my eyes they are the real heroes of comedy. It's one thing to be in front of a TV audience reading from a teleprompt, but it's quite another to perform to a crowd as if your life depended on it. It's a strange feeling of mixed emotions when you walk out on stage and see the front row sitting there with arms folded and 'right then, let's see if you can make us laugh' written all over their faces. On the one hand your heart sinks, but on the other it becomes a great challenge to beat them into submission and change the expression on their faces. These northern guys have spent their whole lives doing that.

We finally got on stage and started working, but because we have done so many TV sketches over the years, I honestly can't remember which sketch we did that night. TV is a hungry beast where comedy is concerned. Once you have performed a sketch, you can't perform it successfully again, because so many people will have seen it the first time. Consequently the turnover of material is huge. In the clubs we could do the same act for years, polishing the laughs to a very high degree. In some ways this is more enjoyable than TV work and is probably the reason why so many comics still 'work the boards' with no real desire to be TV stars.

Live theatre is often better than TV as well because it's such a group experience and it's different every time, even if the core material is the same. Most performers find this so much more satisfying, and audiences do too. What saddens me now is the way that TV can be so powerful and demanding, and when our pantomime bills are topped by names that are known from TV programmes rather than for how good they are as live performers, I think we have gone too far. In the midst of criticism that variety is 'dead', it's still very much alive out there in the theatre, and I would encourage anyone to support this wonderful medium. It will never die, but will just progress through different fashions like everything else.

On stage at the Royal Command we were aware that the audience weren't giving the huge belly laughs that we had become accustomed to, just polite laughter. We thought we were dying, until we finished our act and heard that the other stars were experiencing the same thing. The great British reserve and the presence of royalty kept everything in order.

At the end of the evening we all lined up to be presented to Her Majesty the Queen and the Duke of

Edinburgh. I was next to Anthony Newley and Tommy was next to Joan Collins. It was an unbelievable moment for me. Little Bobby Harper from Oldham was going to meet the Queen! It was an honour that I could never have imagined happening to me. The Queen started coming down the line shaking hands with people and soon it would be my turn. If I said this wasn't the most apprehensive moment of my life then I would be lying. She eventually reached me and I was amazed at how small she was. She even had to look up to *me*! Now that did feel great! She held out her hand and said in a voice that I could hardly understand because she talked so posh, 'Thank you for the hours of enjoyment you and your partner have given us.'

I nodded my head and replied, 'Thank you, Mam.' What an idiot! I'd called her Mam instead of Ma'am, as if she was my mother or something.

I saw a little smile come to the corner of her mouth and she said, 'You are obviously from the North.'

'That's observant,' I thought to myself, but I didn't dare say it. Instead, I just said, 'Yes Ma'am, and very proud of it.'

'So you should be!' she replied and moved on.

After it was all over I could still not believe that I had met the Queen. My grandchildren don't know, and I can't wait for the time when I can sit them down and say, 'Your Granddad met the Queen, you know.' I can just imagine them running to their mother and shouting, 'Mother! Granddad's going senile!'

It was easy to admire the many characters we came across in the business during that successful time. One great moment for me was when I met Eric Morecambe. He was a truly great comic. He wasn't a man who had to

151

be clever or tell a thousand jokes – he just had to look a certain way and people would fall off their seats laughing. We were asked to go to Luton Football Club to meet some kids and when we got there we saw Eric standing in the corridor. It was a magic moment for me and I was astonished to find myself struck dumb. He approached us and held out his hand. It was like meeting a legend, the kind of thing you only dream about. Welcoming us, he said that he found us very funny and that we were a true double act because we had started together and hadn't been 'manufactured'. He was a wonderful man and made me feel very much at ease. My voice came back!

He took us to where the kids were waiting and intro-duced us to them. Because Eric was there I went a bit over the top and started pulling my braces and shouting 'Rock on, Tommy!' The kids were laughing and so was Eric. Then he touched my arm and said, 'Watch, Bobby, this is how you do it.' He slid his glasses to one side of his face as only he could, and the kids went wild. I knew then that I was in the company of the master. I felt as if I was only just learning comedy, and Eric knew so much. We had a drink with him afterwards and then shook hands as we left. I shall never forget that time, as it's very rare to have the opportunity to meet such a comedy genius.

Today I find that comedy has lost what I call 'the belly-laughers' – people such as Tommy Cooper, Max Wall, and many more. I find that comedy has become clever and trendy, and it's not supposed to be, it's simply meant to be funny. I'm not saying that today's comedy is bad; there are some good young comics like Lee Evans, Lenny Henry and Harry Hill. It's just that comedy has changed direction, which may be a good thing in terms of survival, but it's sad not to see anybody belly-laughing at comics any more. People like Eric Morecambe will be sadly missed for some time to come.

Our own career was now flourishing to the point of insanity, but at a time when Tommy and I should have been at our happiest, we weren't. We had everything – a great career, big houses, personal assistants, and no money worries. Money was in such abundance that we could buy literally anything we wanted. One day Tommy was bored and went straight out and bought a boat. Sadly though, despite all we had, we didn't have each other. Our friendship had started to deteriorate.

I really don't know how it started, except that it slowly crept up on us. I began to feel left out of things and the loneliness caused me to become more independent instead of working on being a partner. There was a third person in our relationship now anyway – our manager. It was no longer just Tommy and me, but me, Tommy and the manager. We no longer made decisions between us, but just did what the manager willed. Suddenly Tommy had a new friend in our manager and they would play golf together, go out together, and they even had two flats near each other in London and the same in Spain. When we were in London they would have drinks together and never invited me. It seemed that I was simply pushed out.

I sensed people sniggering and gossiping behind our backs and saying things like, 'Oh, they don't get on you know,' or, 'They hate one another in real life.' The more Tommy became friends with our manager, the more I started to see red. Tommy and I would talk over what we were going to do about certain aspects of our career and

Tommy would tell me what his thoughts were. The next day the manager would phone me and use the exact words that Tommy had used with me the day before. So I came to the conclusion that they were discussing our career without me. Tommy's mind was being taken over, I felt, and a wedge was being driven between us.

I felt increasingly alienated. Even when I disagreed with what the manager was doing I couldn't depend on Tommy to back me up. The biggest thing that hurt me was that even though Tommy looked upon the manager as his friend, I could see that the manager didn't see Tommy in the same way. I would hear him call Tommy names behind his back and it seemed that the manager was just using him to control the act. He knew he couldn't control me, so he must have thought about the 'divide and conquer' technique. Well, he did both, very successfully.

A double act is like a marriage, as each partner has to depend on the other. We had been doing this for years, and knew each other better than anybody else in the world, but now it was spoilt. Instead of a double act it was now a trio, but with me on the outside. During one meeting with the three of us, I suggested something and the manager turned round and said, 'Tommy and I will do the business, you just go into a field and meditate.' This hurt me very deeply, the more so because Tommy didn't stand up for me.

I'd always known about Tommy's insecurities and tried to make him feel important, but now that he didn't seem to need me any more, I ceased to do that. That was wrong of me and I wish now that I had been stronger and held out a hand to him instead of turning away. Things happened over the next few years that caused me great pain and I'm sure that in my own way I caused plenty of the same for Tommy. Little did I know that our manager was stirring Tommy up to an even greater rift between us than I could ever have imagined.

As I drew away from Tommy, he drew away from me. We both felt so insecure, and yet here we were, big celebrities, in great demand, with an audience always waiting to see us. The manager then started telling me that I couldn't write comedy, even though I wrote some of our funniest TV scripts and, with the help of a friend, wrote a cartoon series called *Juniper Jungle* which is still running on TV today. I also wrote all the new material that we would do in the act, but would never perform anything until Tommy had seen it.

Maybe Tommy felt pushed out from the writing, because whenever I gave him a script he wouldn't look at it. I would ask him what he thought of it, hoping that he would offer some input, but the script was usually left in the bottom of his bag. I had spent weeks writing it and his lack of interest made me feel devalued.

I eventually stopped trying to get him involved in the writing process, knowing that whatever I wrote would have to pass the manager's scrutiny, and I wasn't prepared to let that happen. It must have appeared to Tommy at times that I was a control freak who wanted to do everything in the act, but this wasn't true. All I had was our act. I didn't play golf or go off on holidays. I just thought about the act. It became my god.

Maybe I could have looked at Tommy's feelings a little more, but we both had our walls up by then and it would have taken a lot of time and effort to knock them down. Tommy and I had finally lost control of our own lives. We had also lost charge of our money. The accountant took care of everything and just gave us a wage each week. It was like being a little boy again being doled out some pocket money. When we needed any extra money we had to go to him and ask. I began to wish I was back at the factory.

Not only had Tommy and I lost control of events, we had now lost the love that we'd had for one another, and we didn't even share the same dressing room. We hardly spoke. On stage it was different, because Tommy is the best straight man there is and he always sparked me off. I loved working with him, but off stage was something else. It was a sorry state of affairs and we were so unhappy. I frequently wondered why I stayed and didn't just walk away. I looked at Tommy and sometimes felt I had been used. I had given my friendship to him and now he had thrown it back in my face.

Matters reached the point where we could no longer stand each other's company and avoided meeting each other whenever possible. How the public didn't discover this, I shall never know. Maybe we should have got hold of one another and sorted it out before the cancer became too deep, but we didn't. We both had too much pride and blamed one another when in fact we were both to blame. At the same time, we were both hurting very deeply.

Feelings of betrayal fired an incredibly fierce anger within me that I would take out on anybody around me. As I snapped, shouted and cursed at the slightest problem, people soon started to avoid me. They were scared that I would tear them to shreds or hit them. I was the nastiest person to be near, and soon gained a strong reputation for this in the business, particularly after I hit a fellow performer on stage one night. I was very aware that he was upstaging us during our bows at the end of the show and seemed to delight in diverting the audience's attention at the wrong time. This was winding me up and I was becoming increasingly angry. As the front tabs (stage curtains) bounced in I warned him to stop, but he ignored me and when the tabs came in again, I knocked him over. The audience's final glimpse of the show was of the whole company smiling and waving, except one!

My distress at the split with Tommy was very evident and easily spilled over into the lives of others we worked with. Our reputation for being extremely difficult to work with was true, but it was fuelled by a series of lies that were bandied around about Tommy and me. We were under immense pressure both from our success and from the problems we faced in our private lives. I know this is no excuse for abusing someone, but it's the only explanation I can give. If the show wasn't going right, or if people weren't doing their jobs, I would attack them verbally and my words could bring great destruction. I know now that I was wrong to do this and that I should have handled these situations in a different way. I would like to apologize to all the people I hurt and say that I wish I could have had the maturity then that I have now.

On the other hand, I was intensely annoyed at the way people talked about us behind our backs. In this business, gossip is the main source of communication, and people we never even knew were spreading rumours, accusing Tommy and me of all sorts of things. Some people had the guts to come up and interrogate me directly about something bad I was supposed to have done, but many didn't. Gossip is a terrible thing because the majority of people believe it, and before long no one knows what the truth is any more.

The false accusations only served to increase my loneliness and I started to drink very heavily and mess around with other women. Yvonne didn't see me from one day to the next, but if I was working near enough to home I would arrive in the early hours of the morning and stumble into bed beside her. Yvonne used to dread me coming home like this, because in the morning, if any of the family made a noise and woke me, there would be hell to pay. She would spend the whole morning 'walking on eggshells', and was simply relieved when I left the house for the next gig.

My life was in a terrible state and I could easily have contemplated ending it. I had lost my friend and was well on the way to losing my wife and family. Tommy and I no longer travelled together and the only time we met was at the theatre. We had separate dressing rooms and separate hotels.

Then, in 1985, all this changed. We were working at the Bradford Alhambra when a vicar called Max Wigley came into the theatre. He welcomed us to the venue, introduced himself as the theatre's official chaplain, and must have thought it very strange that we were in two separate dressing rooms.

A little later he knocked on my door, and for some reason I let him in. I wasn't a great lover of vicars, and could do without religion, thank you. Max just sat and talked to me, however, and I was surprised that he didn't push God in my face, only talking about his faith when I asked him to. His confidence in a God who loved his creation made me think about my life from a totally different angle.

Over our next few visits to the Alhambra, Max always came to say 'hello'. I started asking him all sorts of difficult questions, trying to trip him up in matters of faith. I was desperate to prove him wrong, because if he was right, then I had some serious thinking to do!

I felt so lost and alone at the time, and was enthralled by the idea that God really knew who I was and really cared about how awful my life had become. Had God given me the gift of comedy that was now the only means of peace and enjoyment I had? Millions of questions circled in my mind, as I continued the daily routine of shows. My internal questions and frustration with life, together with the heavy guilt I was carrying, eventually boiled over and I left the theatre early one night determined to phone Max the following morning. I needed his help to find some answers.

I'm not someone who stays in bed for long. As soon as my eyes are open, I want to get on with my day rather than lying there just thinking about it. This was particularly true the next day, when I awoke half expecting my feelings of the previous night to have dissipated. But no, I still felt in turmoil. I had to come and talk to him, I explained to Max over the phone – right now! Max agreed to see me.

It was still quite early when I arrived at the manse, expecting him to open the door still in his pyjamas. But he was fully dressed and waiting for me, minus his dog collar which I'd always found slightly offensive. This was probably because it seemed to suggest to me that vicars wore this uniform to show that they were better than anybody else. Max had left his off that morning, however, and smiled as I walked into the cosy front room.

We talked for what seemed like hours. Amidst the tears, I poured out all the hurt, fear and guilt that had loaded me down for so long. We prayed, and I finally handed my life over to God. It didn't seem odd; in fact it felt like something I should have done years earlier. I finally felt in touch with myself and my creator. I suddenly had a purpose for living, and the world seemed to be a different place. I had arrived at Max's house totally weighed down by life's problems, and I left feeling as if I could fly. I arrived home exhausted, but free.

Once I had become a committed Christian, I confessed to my wife about my indiscretions. I tried to be sensitive, for I now had a new love for Yvonne, and I didn't want to hurt her. My words stumbled out and she smiled. 'I know what you've been doing,' she said. Everything started to become clear. How could I have tricked my wife about the other women without her knowing? It dawned on me how incredibly patient and loving she had been to me during all the years of agony I had put her through. I believe that it was only through the strength God gave her that she was able to forgive me. Life had changed suddenly from a black-and-white portable TV to a full-colour, wide-screen set. I felt clean, happy and at peace with myself for the first time.

For the next six years I kept my new-found faith close to my chest. I was eager to share my faith with anyone who asked, but never felt the need to shove it down anyone's throat. It was also a time when I wanted to grow spiritually and had many questions that I needed to ask. Dave Berry from the Servants Arts Trust was one of the first people on the scene to bring me spiritual support. He met with me regularly over a period of time and was always ready to pray with me when I felt especially pressurized.

One of the problems I found was that I could never get to church, as I was never in one place for very long. I wasn't a great churchgoer, but I did want to meet others who shared my faith. The charity Christians in Entertainment helped me with that. They specialize in providing emotional and spiritual support for performers while they are on the road, and I found the encouragement, wisdom and help they gave me invaluable. It was my association with this organization that eventually helped me bring my own gospel show into reality. Again, this wasn't an excuse to preach, but simply a way of expressing my faith and following a desire to let others know that God wasn't a boring old man sitting on a throne. We did nine sell-out gigs across the country. It was a fun evening with my band, a crazy pastor called Ray Bevan and Nanette Welmans, a fantastic jazz singer. There was only one person missing – Tommy.

I had already told Tommy about the big change that had happened in my life. We were still not talking, of course, and things couldn't have been worse in our relationship. But now, instead of hating him I wanted to bring back the friendship we had lost so many years ago. I went straight into his dressing room the day after seeing Max and told him that I was now a Christian.

The panicked look on his face showed that he thought I had really gone crazy. Here I was in his dressing room, which was a novelty in itself, but I was also telling him that I'd become a Christian. At least he listened to what I told him and he was clearly glad for me. Amazingly, he didn't rebuke me or call me crazy – he just accepted it. He was obviously well in control of his feelings.

Over the next few weeks I kept looking at Tommy and I could see that he was still hurting. I understood that he wasn't happy and I could now see the good things in him instead of just the bad. I started to reach out to him in whatever way I could, and slowly he accepted me and our friendship started to grow again. Tommy's friendship with the manager started to dwindle as we grew closer once more.

We started travelling together in the same car again and sharing the same hotels. Our peers in show business couldn't believe it when we went back to sharing the same dressing room, because they had become so used to Tommy and me being separate. We started to chat about the years when we hadn't been speaking and eventually, along with plenty of tears, we forgave one another. We cleared out all the hurt and pain of the previous years and started to walk with each other again. A rainbow had appeared, if that doesn't sound too fanciful, and life became good once more. My marriage was strong again, my friendship with Tommy was back, as strong as it had been, and our career was also going from strength to strength.

The act continued to go down well, and the public never seemed to grow tired of our on-stage antics. In between more TV work we topped the bill at the London Palladium, followed by a long summer season, and our career could not have been going better. Our renewed relationship certainly put a new lease of life into our shows. Now that Tommy and I were friends again, the act started to change and we began to have fun on stage, sometimes ad-libbing instead of sticking to our lines.

At the end of our summer season, LWT suddenly decided not to renew our contract after 12 years of constant work with them. This was a huge blow because we were regularly pulling in 10 million viewers. We couldn't understand why they would remove us when we were still in such demand. Then we heard that a new man had taken over as head of light entertainment, and the old saying, 'A new broom sweeps clean,' made sense. We were one of the first to go, along with Jimmy Tarbuck.

From then on variety started to become a bad word in TV circles. It was deemed old fashioned and not what TV was about any more. I think that those who seemed to have the power to tell the viewers what they should watch then began to destroy something of the magic and appeal of TV. To me it certainly became less exciting and the real stars were replaced by cooks and DIY enthusiasts. These programmes were obviously cheaper to produce and left more money for the shareholders, but pure entertainment seemed to vanish.

With our contract with LWT running out, we were approached by the BBC and Yorkshire Television. Although the BBC didn't offer as much money as Yorkshire Television, they would have been a better company to be with because they are loyal to their performers. As usual, however, the manager started talking in our ear and persuaded us to take YTV's offer. It was the worst mistake we made. I'm not saying that Yorkshire Television is a bad company, quite the contrary; it's just that at that time the BBC would have been better for us. I should give Tommy credit here, because he said all along that we were making a mistake and that we should go to the BBC.

We moved to Yorkshire Television and they treated us well, but at the end of the one-year contract it wasn't renewed, and Tommy and I had to move on to other things. The face of TV was now changing across the board and for us it was back to the theatres and clubs. We had enjoyed a TV contract for many years, but to be honest we were pretty tired out from all the hectic recording schedules. Our main fear was that with the demise of Cannon and Ball on TV, our other work might drop away too. TV had apparently made us the biggest draw, but with constant public awareness now gone, would anybody still want us? We began to think that maybe it was time to hang up the costumes. Maybe it was now time to go home.

CHAPTER TEN

DIVORCE AND DESPAIR

In 1979 President Jimmy Carter signed a nuclear peace treaty with Moscow, and Sid Vicious died of a heroin overdose. Teletext and the Sony Walkman were invented as Popeye celebrated his fiftieth birthday. A new Hollywood film, Kramer vs Kramer, *became a box office hit and brought divorce to the big screen. Meanwhile, Tommy was suffering personal dramas of his own and just like the* Kramer *film, his private life was in complete disarray.*

Bobby and I had hit the heights, but our friendship had collapsed. In fact, most of my relationships were at an all-time low and for the next few years, all through the early eighties, I experienced terrific bouts of depression. These deep, dark feelings were something new to me and I found them very frightening. Although at times it seemed almost impossible to go out there and make people laugh, it was probably the focus on my career which kept me from mental breakdown.

One of the worst things that happened was the divorce from my first wife, Margaret. As soon as the news was leaked, I was instantly on the front page of every tabloid paper and it was extremely hard to live with. The whole family came under the scrutiny of the press and were totally exposed for all the world to see. This public humiliation was very difficult to bear.

It was during a long pantomime season at the Bradford Alhambra that I first set eyes on Hazel. A beautiful dancer, or 'hoofer' as we call them in the business, she had just arrived back from working on the cruise ships. She had been away for many months, and when she returned home her mum pointed out this new double act who had just made the big time, Cannon and Ball. Exactly a year later she was one of the dancers in our pantomime. We began a relationship which we both expected to be just a fling, but it spiralled out of control and we fell quickly and deeply in love.

The problem was that we were both married. We had drifted away from our respective partners as show business forced us apart. In our profession, you move around so much that it's nearly impossible to keep a simple friendship going, let alone a marriage. There was no harm meant, but the damage was inflicted bit by bit over a number of years until it was too late to put right. I still liked Margaret, but show business is cruel when it comes to relationships.

I carried a lot of guilt about the divorce and found that it overrode everything I thought or did for a very long time. I needed some space to myself in order to think things through and decided to rent a flat in London. Unfortunately the press followed me back home one night, and having discovered where I lived, they congregated around my front door with cameras at the ready. I was a prisoner in my own home and felt like a man who had committed a vile crime. I didn't understand why the story seemed to attract so much attention, and was at a loss to know how to shake it off. As each day came, I hoped that the onslaught would end, but somehow they just kept dragging me into the tabloids with yet another angle on the same old news. When they couldn't get a particular story they just seemed to make one up. One leading tabloid alleged that I had been partying in London with other women moments after my divorce was finalized and quoted me as saying, 'Right, that's one life over, let's start another.'

These were all lies. I sat in my flat totally alone, breaking my heart. My two girls, Janette and Julie, were heartbroken too, and quite rightly so. They had a dad who was a star and had naturally put me on a pedestal. They were used to seeing the image of a father who was a big success, but in reality here was a father who had been a failure. I suppose that somewhere along the line I was bound to hurt them. I'm just a human being with frailties like everyone else, but to my children I must have been more than that.

I was so guilt-ridden when I was with Hazel that I can't count the number of times she told me to go back home. She thought I didn't love her enough, because I couldn't get rid of this guilt I was carrying and I couldn't start to rebuild my life. Thankfully we stuck it out, and in time created a wonderful marriage together. During the worst times, however, it was the continued success of Cannon and Ball which kept me sane.

The 'no speaking years' proved to be some of the most painful in my life. We started ignoring each other pretty soon after hitting the big time. Although we were playing to capacity audiences, Bobby and I weren't getting on. We had finally made it in the business, and now we weren't even speaking to each other. How sad and silly it all was.

I didn't know Bobby's thoughts in those days and I started a friendship with our manager that was quite terrible for Bobby, who felt I had turned my back on him. Over the next five years we went our separate ways and because we weren't speaking I spent more and more time with our manager. Bobby and I simply didn't agree on anything and I think pride had a lot to with that. Bobby seemed very domineering and wanted to do the act his way, and I began to feel very much the second citizen. We were both hurting each other, and then our manager came between us. I allowed this to happen, and the more Bobby didn't speak to me, the more I leaned on our manager.

I was told many unkind things that Bobby was supposed to have said about me and I believed them. There were times when I think I could have done more in the act but Bobby didn't let me. It really seemed as if he wanted to be the only star of the act. When we were doing the TV show, Bobby would be over in one corner with the script writer discussing what we would do and I would be on my own at the other side of the room just waiting to be told. My humiliation and alienation were all the worse because in earlier times we had been closer than brothers. I understood that everybody looks at the comic to get the laughs, not the straight man, but I wasn't even asked if I wanted to do more. I didn't have ambitions to be the comic – I just wanted the occasional funny line to make me feel more involved; I didn't want to be just the 'feed' all the time.

The general public 'hated' me in a nice sort of way. I was the guy who always picked on little Bobby and was booed. But I wanted to be loved too. When the audience booed me, Bobby would say the act was working. He was right, but I didn't want them booing me, I wanted them liking me. I was jealous of the adoration that the public gave Bobby. When we came out of the stage door the fans would always flock to Bobby first. Yes, it hurt. I began to feel I didn't really belong.

Now that I had a friend in our manager, Bobby found another friend for himself and they opened a nightclub together. I was never asked to join in anything that Bobby did, so I wasn't told about the new club and only found out about it by accident. All my early experiences of childhood rejection came flooding back and I responded by building higher and wider walls around me. Bobby's nightclub was very successful and although I was outwardly glad for him, secretly I wished that I could have been involved too.

Over the next few years, Bobby did lots of things without me. We weren't tied together by an umbilical cord, of course, but after 17 years together in show business there was a natural need to remain close. This just didn't seem possible any more, and we couldn't even pass the time of day with each other backstage, looking the other way if we met in the corridor.

We took extraordinary lengths to avoid one another. On one occasion we had a Sunday concert to do on the other side of the country. We had previously hired a four-seater aeroplane to take us such a distance, but because we weren't speaking, Bobby drove all the way across the country and back and I flew alone. All because of pride. It was sad and soul destroying. On the outside I kept up the pretence of not needing Bobby, and then I went home at the end of the night just breaking my heart. There were times when I wanted to put my arms around him and say, 'What are we doing?'

At other times I could have strangled him. Bobby and I were successful comedians but emotional wrecks.

Then one evening in 1985 Bobby came into my dressing room and smiled at me. I was so used to seeing him frown that I looked away and ignored him, but I sensed something was different. Still smiling, but obviously a bit nervous, Bobby began to speak. Apart from our meetings in the wings to agree what bits of the act to do just before we went on, Bobby hadn't spoken directly to me for six years! Messages were normally sent via someone else.

Surprised, I turned to look at him and there stood another man. I had seen a change in Bobby over the previous few months. He had been cool, not so frantic as usual, and he hadn't been shouting and screaming at other people backstage so much. Muddled thoughts filled my mind. What was going on?

Bobby's voice was gentle but assured, and he told me that he had become a Christian. I was so amazed at Bobby actually speaking to me that I didn't really hear what he said at first. I stood there with my mouth open in astonishment until his words eventually sank in, and then I decided that all the pressure had finally flipped him. Bobby must have gone crazy. On the other hand, he wasn't acting as if he was mental, in fact quite the opposite. Religion was something that I knew very little about, however, so I dismissed his account of what had happened as just another fad. Maybe he would come into the theatre tomorrow dressed in purple?

Over the next few weeks, not only did I notice a significant change in my mate, but more importantly the change remained constant. He became friendly towards me once more and it felt very good after all the years of heartache. Bobby was apparently no longer angry and would sit and talk to me about all sorts of things with an aura of peace about him. He was no longer drunk all the time either, and he talked about his family, something he hadn't done in many years. He told me how important his family were to him now, including his new grandson, whom he hadn't even mentioned before! It was a pleasure having him around again.

As the months passed, our friendship started to heal and I began to open up too. We avoided talking about the years of silence as it was still far too painful to open up that subject, but we discussed Bobby's new-found faith amicably and I knew it was for real. I found that I was jealous of the peace that seemed to surround him and was eager to discover it for myself.

Oddly, it was during this time in 1985 that we were given the honour of being chosen for *This Is Your Life*. Had it been a few months earlier, I don't think the strain in our relationship would have allowed us to go through with it. Bobby and I were on a hectic tour at the time with very few days off. We got a phone call from our manager, telling us that we had to go into London on one of our rare free days to do some filming for one of our TV Christmas specials on LWT.

'There's no way we're doing that!' I said firmly to our manager. 'It's our only day off, so they'll just have to wait until we've finished the tour.'

I can just imagine the shock on his face. Little did I know that the summons to London was planned to catch us for *This Is Your Life*. He couldn't give the game away, of course, and must have been thinking about all the crew and all the work that had been put into the preparation for months – and now here I was, telling him we weren't going to turn up. Apparently my response created mass panic at Thames Television, the makers of *This Is Your Life*, with everybody rushing around saying, 'What are we going to do? They're not coming!'

The manager phoned me back a few hours later and eventually persuaded me that we had to go. I gave in and Bobby and I went reluctantly down to London on our day off.

Sadly, my mother had died by this time and I just wished she had been there to see it, because it was a wonderful experience. Having been told we were filming in Drury Lane, we were instructed to ride a tandem bicycle round to the front of the famous theatre and stop in front of the cameras waiting there. They had stamped 'LWT' on the cameras and had even used our own crew, people we knew, so that we wouldn't suspect. It was cleverly made to look just like a normal shoot, when in fact it was all set up by Thames Television.

We started to pedal our tandem around the theatre and every time we reached the front, David Bell, the director, would stop us and make us do it all again. Bobby and I wondered why we had to keep repeating the action, not realizing that Eammon Andrews, the man with the big red book, was not yet ready to jump out on us. After the third time of being stopped, Bobby and I decided it was time to lighten things up, so the next time round, instead of stopping in front of the cameras, we agreed we would ride right past.

As we approached, David shouted, 'Stop!' but there was no chance, we just kept going. 'Stop! Stop!' he shouted at us. When he realized we weren't going to stop, he threw himself in front of the bicycle. Of course we stopped then, and burst out laughing.

To my right I noticed a huge cannon and saw that someone was sliding out of the barrel. I recognized Eammon with his famous red book, but I still didn't twig. I was too busy laughing at David, who was still prostrate on the ground. Meanwhile, Eammon was trying to slide gracefully out of the cannon and land on his feet, but he fell out and landed flat on his backside. This only made me laugh more, looking at two people on their backs in the street. It must have looked a real fiasco, but then, as smooth and professional as ever, Eammon came straight over to us and said those famous words: 'Tonight, Cannon and Ball ... This Is Your Life!'

Suddenly the penny dropped and I realized it was all for Bobby and myself. A wonderful feeling of exuberance filled me. From the time we walked into the studio to the time we walked out after the show, I never stopped crying. It was a very emotional experience for me. Bobby kept digging me in the ribs and saying, 'Dry your eyes, you tart!' It was one of the most fantastic events of our career.

Our film, *The Boys in Blue*, was made in 1988 and was hugely enjoyable to make because Bobby and I were now speaking. As pals once more we built up each other's confidence, knowing that we both needed encouragement. This was our first movie and we really wanted to do the best job we could.

One of the funny things was that when we got the script, being unused to the way films are shot out of sequence, Bobby and I learned it straight through from beginning to end. This was how we worked with our TV scripts, memorizing hundreds of pages in order, parrot fashion. When we arrived at the set on the first day, feeling like consummate professionals with the first few scenes fresh in our memories, we heard the director say, 'Right everybody! We'll do scene 26.'

Bobby and I looked at each other. What was going on? What was scene 26? We didn't know because we had learned the whole script like a book. We didn't realize that people don't make films like that, but approach it like the bits of a jigsaw and assemble it all together later. We dashed into the trailer and frantically thumbed through our scripts as the make-up lady went into action. Luckily we found scene 26, went on set and acted it out without mishap.

Eric Sykes, Suzanne Danielle, Jack Douglas and the late Roy Kinnear worked on the film with us. We had a wonderful time watching these people work and learned so much from them. Eric Sykes befriended us and would go out of his way to make us laugh, frequently playing tricks that would get Bobby and me into trouble.

One of his favourites was to pull a funny face at just the wrong time. We would be standing on the set waiting for the director to shout 'Action!' It took a lot of work by the director and crew to set a shot up and make sure everything was perfect before the actors were called in. It was a tense moment for us too, as there was always the fear of fluffing lines or not getting the best out of the performance, with our mishaps being stuck on celluloid for ever more.

The director would shout 'Rolling!' to indicate that the film was running through the cameras. Then, just before he shouted 'Action!', Eric would look at me or Bobby with a funny face and we would inevitably break down laughing. The director would come out from behind the camera and ask us why we were laughing. Eric would just stand there with a deadpan face, shrugging his shoulders as if to say, 'It's nothing to do with me.' The director must have been furious with us, but he never showed it, even though we ruined many a shot by our uncontrolled outbursts. Corpsing was never a problem on stage – it could often enhance a comic performance, in fact, because the audience would love the fact that you were enjoying yourself.

Soon after the filming for *The Boys in Blue* was over, we looked forward to our debut at the world-famous London Palladium. It was for an eight-week run with a host of stars, any one of them able to top the bill in their own right. Although we had worked with many international names before, and had appeared at a Royal Command performance and done TV series, to have our own live show with all those wonderful performers was phenomenal. The business side of it was incredible too, with advance bookings breaking box-office records which had stood for 100 years. Bobby and I were doing pretty well, we thought – but we did have our critics.

Critics are an annoying part of the business that you simply have to learn to live with. Very early in our career a pressman came to interview us and afterwards I thanked him. 'Oh, don't thank me, it's just a job,' he replied. 'We're here to build you up and then take you down. It's nothing personal. It's just that we can get more out of you that way.' What he said stuck a deep, fearful chord within me and I never forgot his remarks. They obviously affected my feelings towards the press in the years that followed. The intrusion of the press into your private life can be very disturbing. I even found a newspaper photographer hiding in my back garden one day!

Some critics were particularly harmful, however, the worst being a lady called Nina. She used to evaluate a performance not on the content of the show but on a personal level. This was surely a frustrated woman who wanted to be a celebrity herself but couldn't, so resorted to critiquing others in order to raise her profile a little. I can never understand critics of her calibre. Those who criticize constructively are fine and you can learn from it, but those who try simply to shock and to demean your performance are beyond my comprehension.

For some strange reason we were never loved by the press, which always amazed me because we were so popular with everyone else, filling every venue and drawing millions of viewers. Judging by what was said in the press, it seemed as if the public who came to our shows had got it wrong and the media had got it right. We found this strange and sad.

Foolishly, we thought that we could befriend the media and we invited one critic to a show we were doing in Birmingham. We gave him a meal and a reserved seat with a bottle of champagne on the table. We weren't trying to influence his judgement, we just thought we were being friendly. It was a terrific night; we received a standing ovation and couldn't have gone down any better. We were looking forward to chatting with the critic after the show, because we honestly wanted his opinion, but he never turned up to speak to us. He didn't even leave us a message, although the meal and the champagne had gone.

Two days later he wrote in the tabloids that he thought our act was childish to the point of incomprehensibility. He didn't mention the thousand or so members of the audience who had been shouting, laughing and cheering at us, and he can't have waited to see the standing ovation at the end. Perhaps he had already made up his mind before even seeing the show and wanted an early night. He could have written a fair criticism, but maybe that wouldn't have looked dramatic enough. His story had to be sensational somehow, and I began to feel sorry for reporters who were obviously under increasing pressure not to report the simple truth.

One evening a famous West End critic came to watch our pantomime at the London Palladium. He was known as the 'darling of the West End' and actors would fawn all over him, hoping for a good write-up. Having been to our show, he gave us the worst write-up we had ever had in our lives. He said the show was weak, had no laughs and no plot. This would have been fine if it had been an honest opinion, but he had slept through three-quarters of the show. We knew this for a fact, because Bobby's wife Yvonne sat behind him and watched him fall asleep and wake up just before the end. How scandalous that a man can write such things about something he hasn't properly seen.

It was the press who broke the news that Bobby and I were about to be arrested. The first inkling I had of trouble ahead was when I stood in my kitchen washing up one day and there, peering in at me through my window, was a press photographer.

CHAPTER ELEVEN

THE TAX MAN COMETH

Bobby and Tommy were only too happy to forget the mid-eighties. It wasn't until several years later that the pain which had been pushed deep into their subconscious could be exhumed and discussed. There was some healing to be found in this and the early nineties offered a time of further reconciliation and evaluation. Despite the fact that Cannon and Ball were no longer seen regularly on TV, the public rejection they feared never materialized. Interestingly enough, although the decline in summer seasons and variety shows brought an end to many a celebrity career, Cannon and Ball seemed to continue unhindered. The long seasons in Blackpool beckoned often enough, and Bobby and Tommy found that there were still millions of admirers welcoming their style of humour. They continued to tour the UK and started to travel abroad again, as America opened its arms and they enjoyed their first real overseas success. Cannon and Ball's showboat was soon to be rocked again, however, when another monster surfaced from the darkness of their past. Tommy takes up the story.

It was a warm and windy day, as it often is on the east coast, when our manager met us at the end of the pier in Great Yarmouth. Nonchalantly he told us that he was changing the name of our company because there was a problem that needed sorting out. It turned out to be a good deal deeper and more confusing than that simple statement implied!

Several years previously, we had been advised to set up our own company for Cannon and Ball, in order to keep our accounts easy to manage and to separate us from all the other artistes our management looked after. We readily agreed and as usual went straight back to focusing simply on our on-stage performance. The business side of the partnership was of no interest to us, and we were happy to leave that to the experts.

We signed the necessary paperwork without asking any further questions, and Tommy Cannon Ltd and Bobby Ball Ltd changed to two other names that I honestly can't remember. I then pushed the problem, whatever it was, to the back of my mind, feeling safe to be surrounded by an experienced manager and an accountant we had also had for 20 years. We trusted them with everything and presumed that whatever the difficulty was, they would sort it out.

The matter was forgotten until a few months later, when Bobby and I were called into our manager's office for a special meeting. We were asked to bring our wives, which seemed a strange request. Perhaps we were going to discuss something particularly important about our future?

Both our manager and our accountant were waiting for us when we arrived together, and as soon as we had sat down they dropped the bombshell. 'You owe the tax man a lot of money,' the accountant told us.

'Well, just pay them,' Bobby said, looking first at me and then at the accountant.

There was a quiet moment before our financial adviser spoke again. 'I can't,' he said, 'you've spent it all, you've had everything.'

I couldn't believe what I was hearing, but in the back of my mind I still thought we were going to be all right. 'How much do we owe then?' Bobby asked.

'Well, Bobby owes £90,000 and Tommy owes £100,000.'

I thought I was going to have a heart attack. I didn't know what to do. I certainly didn't have that sort of money knocking around. I felt my wife's hand grip mine and we hung on together for dear life. I just couldn't understand it at all. I knew that Bobby and I had spent a lot, but we had earned a fortune too. The money that had flowed through our hands was ours as far as we were concerned, any tax liability having been removed beforehand – or so we had thought.

Now we were there in front of our manager and accountant who took care of everything, and they were telling us that we were broke. I had always understood that the accountant was paying the tax. Obviously I had been wrong, although I have no idea how the misunderstanding arose. Nothing seemed to make sense, but the bottom line was that we owed an enormous amount of money and had nothing left to give.

It was decided that we would have to liquidate our companies. This meant a form of bankruptcy, but it was the only way we could do it. I felt so bad. I had never been involved with anything like this before and it made me feel like a criminal. I was very worried about the press getting stirred up again and the harmful publicity that all this would create. The future wasn't looking good, and once again it felt as if the life had been knocked out of me. I knew deep in my heart that Bobby and I were on a slippery downward slope. I brought up the subject of adverse publicity and the manager announced that this was the reason for the change of our companies' names.

The liquidation process went ahead slowly over the next 12 months. Meanwhile, Bobby and I put our heads back in the sand and got on with what we did best – entertaining people. We started to cut back seriously on what we spent. The tack was to try to book as many extra gigs as possible, the extra cash going to help pay off some of the debt. This decision only brought us more discomfort, as we ended up working frantically, putting our health in danger and ruining the main motivation for our act, which was simply to make people laugh. Suddenly we were working all hours of the day and night, merely in order to earn as much money as possible. It was all too much to carry, and I wondered on many occasions whether we would survive. There was even worse to come.

We felt bad enough about having to liquidate, but at least, we told ourselves, we would be saved from the distress of publicity. What we didn't know, or weren't told, was that the Department of Trade and Industry were looking into our case and weren't happy about the suspicious-looking timing of the changes to our company names.

Through the DTI investigation the news of our misdemeanour was soon leaked to a hungry press, and we were plastered over every national newspaper. Photographers and reporters followed us everywhere. In some ways I expect this and accept it as part of being in show business. What I don't accept is the invasion of my personal privacy and the privacy of my family. When I saw a photographer jumping over a fence into my garden one day, I knew I'd had enough. I chased the guy out of my property, but not before he'd caught me on camera in exactly the pose of frustration he was looking for. It was a good job I didn't catch him, or I may well have been reported as a mad strangler as well as a 'tax dodger'!

We had no right of reply, of course, but we did hope that the common sense of the readers would help them to see our innocence. The problem is that the public have no real idea of what life in show business is all about, often only seeing the glamour and glitz of it all and assuming we are all millionaires. 'So what if Cannon and Ball owe the Inland Revenue a few thousand? They can surely raise some quick cash by selling one of their homes in Barbados!' In reality, there were no second homes in Barbados, or anywhere else for that matter. We didn't even live in luxurious mansions, just modest family homes. There was no cash either. All that we had been given, like every normal person, we had spent.

Why should our private lives have been scrutinized so much? We never courted publicity like politicians often do, nor had we made claims about personal aspects of our lives and been proven as hypocrites. We just wanted to make people laugh, leave the stage and go back to the privacy of our own homes.

We realized that we couldn't expect any public sympathy if the stories of our misdealings were seen as true. The press bombardment continued, with details of our troubles splashed everywhere. ITN's *News at Ten* announced that the DTI had now banned us from being company directors for three years. The media insinuated that we had tried to fiddle the tax and had been caught. In the eyes of the law, of course, we were clearly responsible. We had signed a document saying that these companies were ours and that we were the directors. Regardless of what else had or hadn't happened, the buck stopped with me and Bobby and no one else. We were branded as losers, cheaters and thieves, and it cut deep.

It was a deeply stressful time, but all we could do was accept the humiliation and meet the looks from people who saw us as tax dodgers with a brave smile. We knew in our hearts that we were innocent. Now that the story had broken and any money we had was taken, there was only one thing left to worry about: we had to try to put the past behind us and press on with our careers. If only it was that simple.

In 1996 we parted company with our manager after 20 years. With all the animosity and suspicion that now existed between us, the relationship was simply untenable. It was a sad goodbye in many ways, but our relationship had run its course.

We also left our accountant that year, but he was extremely reluctant to let us go. We were in Newcastle doing a pantomime and he phoned me up almost every day, saying, 'Look, you don't want to be doing this nonsense. If you leave me now you're going to get yourselves into a lot of trouble.' He pleaded with me endlessly, but after going through liquidation and struggling to clear our debts I saw no reason to keep him on. The case was closed as far as I was concerned, but I didn't know what discoveries still lay ahead.

In 1997, a year after we joined our new accountant, he uncovered documentation that showed we still owed vast amounts of money to the Inland Revenue from a number of different companies with our names attached. Not only that, but we received a letter informing us that an official investigation into our financial affairs was underway. It seemed that the previous matter had not been dealt with properly – it had merely been hidden under the carpet during the liquidation process. The problems that I assumed had been settled returned like an old wound being reopened. I couldn't believe that Bobby and I, two welders from Oldham, were being investigated like villains. It was so frightening that Hazel thought I was going to suffer a heart attack when I heard about it, as I was in such shock that I found it difficult to breathe.

Bobby and I were absolutely clueless about the whole process and looked around for all sorts of people, accountants and tax specialists, to try and sort out the chaos. It was one of the most distressing periods of my life and I felt that our ex-manager and ex-accountant had simply abandoned us, leaving us hanging out to dry. Many a night Hazel and I cried, praying together that we would get through our predicament. It was so degrading. We had to give a full inventory of what we owned, let the investigators look into our bank accounts and justify why we had bought certain items. It was all unbelievable and I was at a loss for words much of the time. Luckily I had my wife's strength, and Bobby's too. Without them I don't think I would have come through it all alive. I finally knew who my real friends were.

It was during this time that a reprieve came, in the form of an offer to go to America. This arrived at just the right time. Not only did it afford us a temporary escape from the pressure of investigation and the prying eye of the press, but it created some space for us in which we could think about our future.

The cracks had started to widen in our relationship with our manager, although he agreed to negotiate the contract to appear at a venue called the Mardi Gras in Orlando. Just days before we were due to appear there, we received a letter stating that our services would no longer be required. They were changing the format of the Mardi Gras show and we would not fit the new style. Legally, the contract was signed and they were bound by it, however. They responded to our protestations by suggesting that we appear at another venue they owned. King Henry's Feast was a theme restaurant where everybody involved was dressed in medieval costume. They had actors who played King Henry and his associates, along with jugglers, court jesters and musicians. Special guest acts were invited to appear and enhance the resident programme of entertainment.

The stage at King Henry's was in the middle of the room and would mean us working 'in the round'. We were used to having all the audience in front of us, not on every side. The essence of comedy is to develop a relationship with your audience, and that's an extremely difficult thing for a double act to achieve in the round. One of us would always have his back to the audience. It's possible that the bookers offered us this difficult venue, secretly hoping that we would back off and release them from their contract. They underestimated the fact that Bobby and I love a challenge – and we needed the money!

I was particularly nervous when we arrived at King Henry's, because the outside of the building was designed as a huge, mock castle. It looked like something right out of *Robin Hood* and was a bizarre thing to find bang in the middle of the USA. Once inside I panicked even more. Stuck in the middle of the main room was an enormous circular wooden stage with tables set all around it, banquet style. We were going to be so close to our audience that I felt it would be like the table-hopping some magicians do in English restaurants. I had an overwhelming feeling that we were going to die the death. Maybe afterwards they would put us in the stocks to finish us off…

We met the manager, who informed us that we too would have to dress in period costume. Although we had dressed in plenty of strange costumes in our time, we just couldn't imagine doing our act with little Bobby Ball dressed as a jester with a pair of red braces attached! Bobby kicked up a fuss and said that he must wear his normal gear because he was going to come in as a tourist and heckle me, just as he had first done so many years earlier. The manager finally agreed, but said that even if Bobby wasn't wearing the period costume, I would have to. Thanks Bobby!

Once it was settled that Bobby would be wearing a tourist outfit and I would be stuck with the dreaded period costume, tights and all, I resigned myself to two weeks of pantomime. The dreaded first night arrived and the scene was set. Standing ready in my ridiculous outfit, I glanced out of the curtains at the audience and did a classic double take. To my horror the audience was made up of nothing but American high-school kids. They wouldn't have a clue who we were, they wouldn't understand the British sense of humour, and the generation gap was huge. I searched for Bobby to share my terrible discovery.

'Bobby, I think we're going to die!'

'Just a minute,' he said, and went to have a look for himself. He came back and lit a cigarette. After what seemed an eternity, he said, 'You're right, but if we're going to go down, we're going to go down big.'

'What do you mean?' I asked, hoping that he had an answer to the problem.

'You'll see,' was all I got back.

Bobby left to stand ready at the back of the room, and I nervously adjusted my costume. I could hear the other actors and knew that I would be on very soon. Now that we'd changed the act, it meant that I would be starting on my own, something which I hadn't done for many years. By this time I was a mass of nerves. Suddenly I heard my name being called and before I knew it I was in the centre of the round platform.

The audience looked up at me as if I was from another planet. It was understandable, because for the last hour they had been entertained by people talking Old English and singing songs like 'Greensleeves'. Suddenly here was this guy in tights and a kind of a smock with a leather belt tied around the middle, singing a modern romantic song! It was like pantomime time on Planet Ga-Ga.

I carried on regardless and just as they started to lose interest the back doors flew open and there was Bobby. Phew! Was I glad to see him! He was dressed in a Mickey Mouse baseball cap, a Mickey Mouse T-shirt and the longest shorts, or the shortest longs, I have ever seen, with a blow-up whale tucked under his arm. Bobby started to shout at me from the back of the room and everyone went quiet as he proceeded to walk through the audience, hitting people over the head with his plastic whale. They had never seen anything like this in their lives. He eventually reached the stage and we did the rest of the act as normal. The place went wild, and at the end all the kids stood up and started chanting our names. It was a fabulous night, and for the first time in many months I felt physically and emotionally better. The success of the evening was like a tonic running through my veins and couldn't have been more heaven sent.

Arriving back in England for our pantomime season, we were both full of confidence in the act, though nervous about how the Inland Revenue investigation was proceeding. As usual we put all our energy and efforts into the show, determined to block out the worry by having a good time on stage, and looking forward to celebrating Bobby's birthday during the pantomime run.

Bobby is a gadget man, and he just loves anything unique and unusual. When he gets a new 'toy' he will often show it off to everyone, but he also gets bored with it pretty quickly when the surprise element has worn off. The previous year I had bought him a Dictaphone that was also a personal alarm clock, a radio and a calculator. Why someone would need all these things at once beats me! I wanted to call him 'Inspector Gadget', but someone else made the name famous before me.

Birthdays have always been special occasions for Bobby, who loves the surprises that seem to happen when it's his turn to celebrate. Every year someone would try to find a different way to shock him, and he never knew which direction it would come from. During our previous pantomime at the London Palladium, the grand finale included a huge prop horse that would fly down with the princess riding grandly on its back. On

Bobby's birthday night we were nearing that scene when we heard the audience laughing. They weren't supposed to laugh just then, because this was a big, spectacular moment. Bobby turned round to see what was causing the commotion, and there was his wife Yvonne on the horse, wearing the princess's dress and being lowered down from the ceiling. She was holding out her wand as if she had been acting the part all her life. The entire cast started cheering because they knew that Yvonne was doing this for Bobby's birthday.

Everything was going well, when suddenly the mechanism that lowered the horse stopped and Yvonne was stuck in midair. Her face was a picture and she clearly didn't know whether to laugh or cry. The audience laughed even harder, because they could see that something was wrong.

Bobby stepped forward and told the audience that it was his birthday and that the lady on the horse was his wife. I looked at Yvonne and she was getting more and more embarrassed. She just sat there trying to wave to people as if nothing was wrong. This was Yvonne's present, Bobby went on, but something had gone wrong and she was now stuck in midair, and we were going to leave her there all night. The audience roared in approval and Yvonne glared at Bobby, obviously wishing that looks could kill.

Bobby insisted that everyone exit the stage, leaving Yvonne dangling. The audience started to applaud her as she stared out into the darkness while the curtains closed. We all came back on stage to help her down and Bobby gave her a huge kiss. I felt really proud of her myself for attempting to do a stunt like that, because deep down Yvonne is a very shy person. Needless to say, she never did anything like that again!

ROCK ON, TOMMY!

This particular year I wanted to do something different to surprise Bobby that would top what Yvonne had done. Eventually I settled on the idea of a kissagram. He had never had one before, and I thought it would be a wonderful surprise and a great laugh. How wrong I was! I phoned the agent and told him that I wanted a kissagram to come to the theatre, walk on stage, kiss Bobby and give him the present that I would provide. He said he would arrange everything.

The night of Bobby's birthday came and everybody was congratulating him backstage at the theatre. I could see that Bobby was giving me strange looks as if to say, 'Where's my present, Tommy?' I pretended I'd forgotten it and would give it to him the next day. He accepted this and we went on stage. The theatre was packed with mums and dads and kids – it was a great atmosphere. Bobby was feeling higher than usual, it being his birthday, but I was a little nervous because the kissagram hadn't turned up yet and it was nearly curtain up time.

Just before the interval, Bobby and I were on stage playing the two robbers from *Babes in the Wood* when people started laughing in the wrong places. Bobby and I turned around to find a gorgeous kissagram girl standing behind us. I looked at Bobby and he was laughing because he immediately twigged that this was my birthday surprise and he appreciated it. Then suddenly the band started to play 'The Stripper'. Bobby's face dropped and so did mine. This was *not* what I had expected. They must have sent a strippagram instead!

The girl started to take her clothes off and was going for it in a big way. Everybody on stage just stood there open mouthed. Even the audience had sunk into a deathly hush. The auditorium was full of kids and on stage was a woman stripping for Bobby. Imagine the picture! Bobby never moved; he was rooted to the spot. I pulled myself together and signalled desperately to the stage manager to close the curtains, which he did as quickly as possible, just before she was totally nude. The girl just kept on stripping. She thought she was doing a great job. I grabbed one of the dancers' robes from the wings and flung it around her, thanking her for what she had done. She thought it had been marvellous and told me she had never been on a stage that big before, and she thought she had gone down well. She's obviously never been to a pantomime before, I thought to myself...

When she had left the building I went to apologize to Bobby, who was still rooted to the spot. He couldn't believe what had just happened, but started laughing as I approached. He'd never seen anything as funny as the expression on my face when she'd started stripping, he said. How he wished he'd been able to take a picture. Certainly no other pantomime in this country ever ended the first half in such a startling way.

After the interval we went back on stage and made a joke about it to the shocked audience and soon had them laughing again. Of course it hit the press, and they had a field day with headlines like 'Cannon and Ball in Kiss Me Quick Panto'. I was so embarrassed. That was my first and last experience of kissagrams.

The months of the investigation continued with an eerie silence into the spring. There seemed to be no end to the black cloud that hovered above us, and it affected everything we did. The good news was that we had been so well received in the States that they had invited us

back for another summer. I hoped that this time would
be as good as the last, but secretly wondered how much
longer we could cope with the intense pressure that
followed us unavoidably wherever we went.

CHAPTER TWELVE

A GREAT LOSS

Ironically it was the time Bobby and Tommy spent in this foreign country, several thousand miles from home, that restored their flagging self-worth. Away from the burden of worry, they flourished once again as an act that was confirmed as unique and outstanding. The old adage, 'A change is as good as a rest', certainly proved to be true for the boys as they spent another summer in the sun, a summer which created an oasis for Bobby to rethink his past and prepare for his future. Nonetheless, he was still dogged by the cloud of despair that hung over him during the long tax investigation.

The times in America were magical, especially when we were booked to appear at The Tupperware Center in Florida. It sounds like a gag, but was actually the headquarters of the giant food container company and contained a huge, 2,000-seater theatre which was very popular amongst locals and visitors alike. I expected the venue to be made of plastic with a huge lid that lifted off, but it was much nicer than that! We had been booked for a three-month contract, so Tommy and I took our families and settled in. Renting two houses, we started to live like Americans, and I would get back from the theatre at about 10 o'clock at night to find Yvonne in the giant hot tub with a glass of wine in one hand, looking like a film star.

The time at Tupperware was good, but we weren't dragging too many people in as we were relatively unknown in America. Expecting to return home early, we were pleased when another venue approached us and offered to take us on for the remainder of our contract. The invitation was to appear at the world-famous Grand Ole Opry in Nashville, which was something of an honour because only a handful of English comedians have ever performed there.

My introduction to Nashville was to be one of the strangest experiences I have ever had. Not knowing what to expect when we arrived at this famous city, I couldn't believe my eyes when I saw the cabby ready to transfer us from the airport. He was dressed in a full cowboy outfit, complete with boots and spurs, and looked as if he'd just come off the set of a John Wayne Western. He removed his stetson and in the cowboy twang that's so prevalent in Nashville said, 'Where would you nice folks like to be taken to?' He was a gentleman. Tommy named the hotel and we set off.

Just to make conversation, I asked him, 'Are there many song-writers in Nashville?'

'The place is goddamn full of 'em!' he snapped. 'Everybody's a goddamn song-writer!'

The atmosphere in the car had suddenly changed. This gentleman had become irritated. To make light of the situation, I went on, 'So you don't write songs, then?'

'Sure do,' he replied, stopped the car, got out and ran round to the boot. Before we knew it he was back carrying about six cassettes. 'What do you boys want to hear?' he said getting into the car. 'Old country or new country?'

'Anything really,' I replied weakly, wishing now that I hadn't asked him. He put a cassette in the player. 'This was a song I wrote in '72. It's about Vietnam.'

He continued to play us his songs and provide a running commentary about their meanings for the whole trip. When we reached the hotel we got out with some relief, and he put his head out of the car window. 'Well, what do you boys think about my songs?'

'Er … very good,' Tommy replied politely, not quite knowing what else to say.

'Yahoo!' shouted the cabby. 'At last, somebody who likes my songs! This fare is on me my boys, and y'all enjoy yourselves whilst you're here in Nashville, you hear?' Then he was gone and Tommy and I just looked at each other and burst out laughing. What a mad place. And it was true – everybody in Nashville was a song-writer, or so it seemed.

Work in the USA continued and we enjoyed some sunshine months in a rural town called Branson in Missouri. During our time there, Tommy was invited to judge a pig-calling contest. Everyone who entered had to make the sound of a pig squealing. The pigs were supposed to recognize the call and run to their respective owners. It sounds crazy, but it's true. Tommy judged well, and along the way learned the essential art of pig-calling. I joked that Tommy would be able to get any man's pig back, for years afterwards.

Branson boasts 36 theatres within a radius of three miles, with some of the venues being owned and worked by stars such as Kenny Rogers, Andy Williams, The Osmonds and Glen Campbell. The area attracts millions of tourists a year and many of the theatres do up to five shows a day. We were booked to appear at the Will Rodgers Theater, and although the audiences were small we did really well. Off stage we filled our days with golfing and sailing, and after the show enjoyed meeting the other stars who were appearing there. It was like a holiday, and even though our tax problems were still brewing at home, I had a lot of good things to look forward to.

When we left England Joanne was pregnant again, so I was excited by the idea of having another grandchild to enjoy when I returned. But then we got a phone call to say that my daughter had suffered a miscarriage. She was 11 weeks pregnant when it happened and Yvonne and I felt so sad for her, sharing her sense of loss. Yvonne and I wept over the problem of being trapped in America when we wanted to be at home supporting her. God is good, though, because not too long afterwards she was blessed with a beautiful little boy called Sam.

About two weeks after hearing of Joanne's miscarriage I had a phone call from my sister telling me that our mother had been taken into hospital and was critically ill. Mam hadn't been well for a long time, but to know that she had been rushed into hospital was a big concern. I was overcome with worry and didn't know where to turn. I told Tommy and the owners of the theatre that I was going home, and they agreed under the exceptional circumstances to let me do that. The only tickets Yvonne and I could get were for the following day, and we packed our bags in anticipation. I found I couldn't relax. I was desperate to get home and hold Mam's hand.

Later that afternoon I went to the shops, and when I got back Tommy was waiting for me. He held me close to him and said simply, 'Bobby, your mother has passed away.'

I can't begin to explain what I felt, except to say that I was filled with an intense feeling of loss, as if something vital had fallen away. I suppose I never expected my mother to die, somehow. We think that our parents will be here for ever, and when they're suddenly gone we can't comprehend it. I sat down on the steps leading up to our back door and wept uncontrollably. Yvonne sat down beside me and hugged me. She was a great comfort, but at that moment nothing else mattered except the loss I felt. America, success, tax problems – none of these seemed important. I just felt numb, as if a part of myself had just died.

Yvonne and I flew back to England the next day as planned, not to see my mother in hospital but to bury her. As we took off, a million thoughts swirled around my head and I felt guilty that I hadn't been there when she died. The very fact of her death also brought home to me my own mortality. We all experience different things in life, but one thing that every human being will experience is death. I considered my faith once more and, flying high above the clouds, reflected on what heaven might be like. It made me consider that nothing in this world really matters except God and your family. Everything else is merely cosmetic.

When I got back home, I hugged my sister Mavis. Dad had died several years previously. Mavis had been wonderful during my mother's illness and even now she was being strong for me. She's a wonderful human being. We buried my mother in a tiny graveyard outside Oldham, and I returned to Branson to finish off the contract. It was never quite the same for me after that, however, and I was continually homesick. I just longed to get back home for good. Maybe I wouldn't have wished so hard if I'd known what was waiting for us there.

If anyone had tried to predict the episode that was to follow, I would never have believed them. Within three months I went from being totally ignorant of financial law to having an understanding I never thought possible. A new side of Bobby Ball emerged as we arrived back in England and were soon immersed in a cesspool of complicated legalities which only seemed to get deeper and deeper.

Soon after our initial meeting, our new accountant had written to our previous consultant, advising him of his new appointment to the partnership and requesting, as required by professional ethics, that he be permitted to act on our behalf. The reply he received said that there was no objection to the changeover, but the books and records would be withheld until an outstanding invoice had been settled.

A search at Companies House at this time also revealed that one of the previous companies, Cannon & Ball Entertainments Ltd, was still listed. Incredibly, this meant that because Tommy and I had already been disqualified, there was nobody actually controlling the company. Companies House acknowledged that they were possibly wrong to accept forms of resignation without at least a further director and company secretary having been elected, but said they were under no obligation other than to process the forms at face value.

Tommy and I were at a loss to explain why the company hadn't been struck off, which was what we had understood would happen. Tommy recalled the apparent immediacy of the ruling several months earlier, and the urgency with which all the company cheque-books were to be destroyed. Although we didn't understand much about what was going on, past experiences were now beginning to drop into place. Something certainly hadn't been done right.

Tommy also remembered that only after speaking to our financial adviser back in June 1996 had we discovered that cheques were still being drawn against the company's bank account – after the date of the disqualification. This was particularly worrying because the bank still held the deeds of both our houses as collateral for a loan. Although this loan had been repaid, the deeds of our properties had not been recalled, which naturally hadn't sat too happily with Tommy and me at the time.

Our new accountant asked for an explanation regarding the delay in striking off the company, and was told that final accounts had yet to be prepared. It became obvious to us that our old accountant knew we were in deep trouble and wanted to avoid dealing with these difficulties himself.

Believing that vital information was being withheld, our new accountant felt it was necessary to review the company's books over a longer period. A request was made for all the records held by our previous accountant to be forwarded. The reply argued that it was better for him to attend to the continuing affairs of Cannon and Ball, as there was not much left to do apart from tidying up the deregistration and looking after the formal removal of our old company from the Register. It was obvious that our old accountant still wasn't going to let go without a struggle.

Our new financial adviser expressed surprise that there should be any further work required. With no director to sign for the company, surely this would indicate to the Registrar that it was no longer operative and by default he would have to strike the company off, without needing further instructions. Tommy and I looked at each other. Were we supposed to understand all this?

Our previous accountant continued to refuse our requests for information until all outstanding invoices were settled. On 13 February a letter from him made a reference to an Inland Revenue investigation that had been 'going on for some time'. The news slipped like a bad penny into a slot machine, jamming up the works. It all started to make sense.

Show business is such a strange profession with so many hidden corners that high earners in the business are prime targets for the Inland Revenue. Sadly, this often involves artistes who have no idea how to handle that side of things. We tried not to let the thought of an IR investigation worry us, however, as we assumed there was nothing to fear. Tommy had bravely said, 'We have nothing to hide, so let's have a meeting with them.' How foolish we were.

Our new accountant felt, as did Tommy and I, that serious and genuine questions needed to be answered, and he had an obvious and natural desire to have sight of the company books and records in order to find some of these answers. We then discovered recent documents which showed that our company's management accounts had in fact been drawn up for the final period. Although these papers had been filed with the Inland Revenue, neither Tommy nor I, despite being both directors and shareholders, had ever signed them, either in draft or final form. A copy was duly faxed to our new accountant by the relevant tax office. He sent back a note confirming that these final accounts were indeed in existence, but we weren't in a position to establish whether or not they were a true reflection of the business. The tax inspector had commented to our new accountant that he had wondered why these documents were unsigned!

Shortly after this, writs were issued by our previous accountant for the recovery of his unpaid invoice. We immediately settled the debt without query, even though neither Tommy nor I wanted to pay him as we had questions over some of the work he had done. The comfort now, however, was that there was no reason why anything should be withheld any longer. Nonetheless, we were in fear of what we might find when the old accounts eventually arrived, and each day we felt like tiny ants, struggling to carry a weight 50 times bigger than ourselves.

While we waited for 'the day of the boxes', we decided to make a direct approach to the tax office. But first we needed to find someone who could help us through the legal minefield we were now facing. The tax specialist Neville Goodwin, previously a tax inspector himself, said that he would be delighted to help. Without mentioning any names, we gave him a broad outline of the case, the difficulties encountered, and our new accountant's concern that the Revenue's Special Compliance Office (SCO) might be involved due to the likely scale of the investigation. Our initial half-hour introductory meeting soon extended into a full day. I wondered how much all this would cost, then reminded myself that this was not as important as paying our dues and clearing our names.

We agreed that our accountant should call the SCO in Manchester, and very soon after that a Mr Andrew Shaw was on the line, very interested to know who our new accountant was and that he wished to discuss this long-running case. A meeting was arranged for that same week and both Andrew Shaw and a Mr Chris Oates were there to greet us. Chris Oates introduced himself as Group Leader at SCO Manchester, and Andrew Shaw explained that he was from the Inland Revenue's Accounting Standards unit. This was a whole new world to us, and we'd obviously got the big boys on our case.

The meeting seemed to go well and everyone remained cordial throughout. It transpired that the Inland Revenue had begun their investigation back in 1990, and our new accountant feared that this would inevitably lead to prosecution.

I looked at Tommy's knees to see if they were shaking as much as mine. The strange thing is, our fear was based on feelings of inadequacy and helplessness in a situation which we didn't understand. We felt like pawns in a game of chess, being moved around the board by other people's hands. We were never afraid of being found consciously guilty, because we knew right from the start that we were innocent. We hadn't set out deliberately to dodge any tax payments. All I really cared about was justice. I was angry that we might be seen as guilty for something we hadn't done, and what terrified me the most was the thought of losing complete control over my own life.

By this time in the meeting Tommy and I felt as if we were drowning in a sea of figures, statements and points of law, and we didn't know which way to turn. We were simple comics who had somehow been caught up in this incomprehensible tidal wave and dragged along. I couldn't believe that I had brought my wife and family down into such a mess through my naivety. I'd had the world at my feet, and now I was facing a possible jail sentence. How the mighty had fallen.

Neville requested that Tommy and I and all other parties involved meet for a 'full and frank confession to all irregularities' under the 'protection of a second Hansard'. This was all gobbledygook to Tommy and me, and we just sat there staring blankly at each other. The Revenue were unable to agree immediately to this Hansard, since they had never before, as I understood it, allowed a taxpayer more than a single opportunity to grasp the olive branch, so to speak. Fortunately they eventually agreed that such an offer could be made.

When the Inland Revenue offered us a second Hansard, I didn't even know we had been offered a first one. I didn't even know what a Hansard was. Fortunately, of course, our advisors did, and slowly and considerately they began to help us understand what was involved.

'Hansard,' they told us, 'refers to a statement practice carried out by the Board of the Inland Revenue in relation to the institution of criminal proceedings for serious fraud against it.' Wow! Now I really had to concentrate! 'It's the practice of the Board that it may accept a money settlement instead of instituting criminal proceedings against the taxpayer, but they do reserve full discretion in all cases as to the course they take, and won't emphatically rule out criminal proceedings even if they accept a cash settlement and the taxpayer cooperates fully with the case. In practice, proceedings will seldom commence where the taxpayer makes a full confession and allows the Inland Revenue ready access to all records and information sought.'

It basically meant that if we were prepared to be totally open and honest, the Revenue would look favourably on our case. This was no problem to us, but Tommy and I were obviously in big trouble. We hadn't got a clue about most of what they were talking about, and we hadn't been remotely aware of the seriousness of the case against us. At the end of the day, it was down to Tommy and me, because we were the company directors. There was no way round that. My blood went from boiling with anger to freezing with worry.

Shortly after our initial meeting with the Revenue, the books and records arrived from our previous accountant, although still nothing was included in relation to the old limited companies. A further request for the remaining information was made, with the added advice that the Inland Revenue were investigating us and that there was no legal reason to withhold anything. The books followed by return.

On receipt of these boxed records, however, a number of records appeared to be missing. Bearing in mind that enquiries began in the early 1990s, we had anticipated a vanload of information running back to at least the mid-eighties. What arrived were bank statements dating back to September 1995, purchase invoices from October 1995 and PAYE records for 1993/94 through to 1996/97. A sales daybook, purchase daybook and cash book were also part of the package, but where was the rest? Nobody could explain how the records went missing or whose fault this could have been.

Further enquiries were duly made, but nothing more was forthcoming and the Revenue accepted that our accountant's investigation report would inevitably require best estimates in place of the missing information. This possibly assisted the reporting function, but it was also to our misfortune, as in all probability we would now have to pay more than we actually owed, given the guesswork involved.

Further meetings and correspondence passed until late September 1997, when efforts by our accountant culminated in a further meeting between Tommy, Hazel, Yvonne and myself, along with Neville Goodwin and the two tax officers in Manchester. It was explained to us at this meeting that the taxation affairs of Tommy and me and of the various companies under our control had been referred to the SCO in 1990 because a number of irregularities had arisen in the accounts, indicating that incorrect personal tax returns had been filed. Tommy and I reflected in our minds on the years of signing documents which we were never able to understand fully ourselves as they were so complicated.

It was also disclosed at this meeting that Tommy and I had been offered a Hansard in 1991 via our previous accountant, in order to disclose the irregularities and sort the matter out. To our knowledge, no disclosures were made at that time and in 1992 our companies were placed into liquidation. In 1994 our successor companies Momentschems Ltd and Indexoption Ltd were also placed into liquidation. We were shocked to hear that all four companies had substantial tax arrears. We were going to be buried.

As an indication of our willingness to cooperate fully with the Revenue, payments on account of the alleged underpayments were required, and Tommy and I each handed across the table a cheque for £50,000. Yvonne made me laugh by asking whether her cheque guarantee card was needed! To raise the money we had to remortgage our homes, cash in our retirement pensions and life assurances and sell whatever we could. Yvonne and I ended up with nothing, not even enough to buy a decent meal. Well, she did marry me for better or worse … and at that moment it certainly seemed to be all worse. What followed can only be described as even more heartbreaking and degrading.

Internal photographs were taken of every room in our homes, and others of our furniture and our cars, to show what kind of lifestyle we were enjoying. I can remember Yvonne sitting in a corner watching all this, feeling so invaded and looking so sad. It broke my heart. When the photographers left Yvonne broke down crying and said she felt as if she'd been raped. It was a very traumatic time, but it didn't stop there. Detailed questioning followed about our business and private affairs and the amounts of cash we carried. After giving the tax man £50,000 each, Tommy and I were lucky if we carried a fiver!

They asked us if we owned any safes, requested details of old and current bank accounts, both offshore and onshore, and asked if we were involved in any money market dealings. Tommy and I just laughed. We couldn't fill in our own tax returns, let alone deal on the money market. Investments and credit-card spending, details of current and previously owned cars, boats and property, inheritances, all these were carefully investigated. When all the information had finally been amassed, Neville and our accountant passed it to the investigating officers.

Even though it was a horrendous experience, Tommy and I began to understand how all this was relevant to an Inland Revenue investigation. 'A model of lifestyle and spending is created and then equated to declared earnings, thus establishing whether and, if so, how much additional income there must have been to afford the same.' I was even beginning to understand the jargon!

Neville and our accountant were wonderful in the way they reassured and comforted us throughout this difficult time, and at our next meeting with the Revenue we were similarly reassured when two trays of sandwiches appeared along with pots of coffee and tea at lunchtime. Apparently this isn't the usual policy of the Revenue while undertaking an enquiry, and it seemed that although Tommy and I undoubtedly owed a great deal in unpaid tax, it was accepted that we hadn't set out to be wilfully fraudulent. As company directors, however, we were now fully aware that we had been under legal obligation to oversee the running of our companies, and that we had been naive in not putting ourselves in a position to do so. Our accountant felt that it would be difficult for the Revenue to maintain any claim that Tommy and I were aware of the unpaid liabilities, since there was no evidence to suggest that we were actually in control of our own companies' finances.

The Revenue advised our accountant that the sum of unpaid tax and national insurance was, to their knowledge, somewhere between £300,000 and £400,000. There was also likely to be interest and penalties on top of that. All in all, Tommy and I were possibly facing total personal debts of around £700,000.

We were also aware that the actual unpaid income tax and national insurance might well be more than the estimate above, though nothing specific had yet been put to us by the Revenue. There was a difficulty in establishing which of our various companies may have owned assets over the years which had been used in a personal capacity by Tommy and me. Were there a number of 'benefits in kind' which were yet to be assessed? Again, Tommy and I just didn't know. We were completely at the Revenue's mercy. Other tax arrears of almost £27,000 also appeared on the final accounts of Cannon & Ball Entertainments Ltd, dated 13 May 1996.

The investigation report was completed by Neville and duly signed by Tommy, Hazel, Yvonne and myself as former directors. The Revenue accepted everything and an offer was made by our accountants to settle the outstanding liability. After deliberation the Revenue came back to us with the news that they didn't consider it to be a sufficient amount. In the summer of 1998 they finally asked for an inclusive £250,000, which we all agreed on.

This amount was to include everything, both known and unknown liabilities, all tax, national insurance, Section 419 interest on overdrawn directors' loan accounts, interest and penalties. Tommy and I were pleased with the outcome, considering that initially we were looking at a possible £700,000, and somehow we also felt justified. We had been victims of our own naivety. As we had already paid £100,000 between us, the Revenue agreed that we could spread the remaining £150,000 over three years. It was also agreed that the company Cannon & Ball Entertainments Ltd could be finally wound up and removed from the Register. The saga was over.

The £150,000 liability was a huge amount to find, even though it was spread over three years. Considering that now we didn't have a penny to our names and that we would still have to pay 40 per cent tax on all our future earnings, how would we ever find an extra £25,000 each on top to pay this off each year? We faced a huge financial struggle, but it was better than the potential consequences of not having cooperated. These were unthinkable; the alternatives were disastrous and may even have included a prison sentence.

The reports of our failings were once again plastered all over the press. To hear our names on the news and see them spread all over the tabloids alongside insinuations that we were fraudsters was hard and humiliating for us and our families. It just wasn't the whole truth. We still had no right of reply, and just had to hope the public would believe the best of us. Sadly not all of them did, and one day we were leaving after a show when we were confronted by a guy who said to us, 'Well, you two have come down a lot, haven't you? You should have paid your tax, then you wouldn't be in this mess. Serves you right!' All Tommy and I could do was smile and tell ourselves he wasn't to know the truth. When we got into the car Tommy put his arm around my shoulders and said, 'Never mind, Bobby, the gigs have given us a little more to pay our tax off.'

Sadly, when all this hit the press a lot of Christians turned their backs on us. I found this hard to understand, because one of the biggest joys about Christianity is people not judging others. Although everyone gets it wrong at times, forgiveness is always waiting just around the corner. People should certainly look at their own lives before condemning anyone else.

Yvonne and I had friends who would regularly telephone and write. When our problems were reported in the press, however, several friendships fell silent. We had been judged on what was written in the papers. My faith took a pounding during that difficult time, because I didn't expect Christians to behave like that. The support, understanding and forgiveness I had hoped for from some areas of the church never came, but I managed to stand strong with God and he taught me that everyone is fallible, even Christians. Life's strange, isn't it?

As the old saying goes, 'Time is a great healer', and from my own experience I believe this to be true. Tommy and I later found that we were able to forgive our previous manager and accountant, and we hoped that they would one day be able to forgive us for some hurtful things we had said and done in return. We even started to hope that some day we could all meet again, put whatever went wrong to rest, and be able to laugh together about the good days.

CHAPTER THIRTEEN

HORSES, HOLES AND HIT MEN

With their financial worries behind them, Bobby and Tommy were now free to enjoy a normal life once again. Whilst Bobby continued to let his imagination run riot, churning out a million ideas a second, Tommy worked hard to retain his physical fitness. Always an active man and a lover of sport, he started regular workouts at the local gym and took every opportunity to pursue his favourite hobby.

Golf has been my biggest source of relaxation over the years and my mentor is a guy named Gilliam Hardiman. He's the pro at the old links in Blackpool, one of the nicest men I have ever met, and he taught me the rudiments of the great game. Playing golf has given me some fantastic memories and I count myself lucky to be part of a show business fraternity that has fun on the golf course and raises millions of pounds for charity at the same time. We regularly have pro-am events and these have given me the chance to play with some of the greatest golfers in the world. What a wonderful thing to have happened to me. I'm just a guy from the back streets of Oldham, and I'll be able to say to my grandchildren, 'I've played golf with the legends of the game, you know.' Of course, they'll say in reply, 'Grand-dad's going potty!' and just to prove it, I'll take out these letters to show them.

Dear Tommy,
I just wanted you to know how much I enjoyed playing with you in the BBC tournament at Turnberry. It was great fun, particularly since we won our match. I under-stand that the BBC is happy with the results and I hope that their viewers will enjoy the tournament on televi-sion. Perhaps we will be doing it again sometime. In any event, I hope our paths will cross in the future.

Best personal regards.

Arnold Palmer.

Another letter also has a special place in my heart.

Dear Tommy,
I just want to tell you again what a pleasure it was play-ing with you in the BBC Pro-Celebrity. What a par 5 you played! You made the hole look like a short par 4, and what a putt on the final hole.

Take care, my friend,

Gary Player

These are the kind of memories that stay in your head for ever, and I'll enjoy recalling them when I'm sitting in my old man's rocking chair somewhere. I don't just play with professional golfers, either, and one of my partners has invariably been Frank Carson. I use the term 'partner' loosely, here, because I could be on the ninth hole and Frank could be on the twelfth and I would still hear him talking. There's a saying in show business that you should never lock eyes with Frank, because if you do you won't get away and Frank will talk you to death. The most popular joke about Frank amongst other comics goes like this:

Q. *'What's the difference between Frank Carson and the M1?'*
A. *'You can turn off the M1!'*

For all that, though, Frank's a great bloke and a great comic. After so many years, and now well into his seventies, he's still making people laugh. That's the best accolade a comic could have.

Amongst the comics I admired, no one was a greater character than Les Dawson. He was a one-off. For one pro-am in Scotland there were quite a few guys from show business playing, Les included. We went up there for the weekend and were due to travel back on the Monday morning. All the performers from Manchester travelled up in the same aeroplane and the journey was crazy. When a bunch of comics get together, the laughter never stops. Frank Carson was with us too and he didn't stop talking for the whole flight.

We duly arrived in Scotland, played the game and then let our hair down at the hotel over a drink or two. It's a well-known fact that Les liked a drink and that night was no exception. He made everyone roll about in hysterics all evening, while he got slowly plastered. It was about 4.30 in the morning by the time we decided to head for bed. Our plane was leaving at 9 o'clock, so there weren't many sleeping hours remaining.

As I left the lounge I saw Les still sitting in the hotel reception, blitzed out of his mind (the rest of us weren't far behind him). 'Tommy!' he slurred. 'Will you give me a call in the morning?'

'Of course I will, Les,' I said, knowing his fear of missing a schedule. 'We're all going back on the same plane anyway.'

'No, Tommy,' he continued. 'It's important that I catch that plane because I have to go to London tomorrow afternoon to record *Blankety Blank*.'

'Les,' I replied firmly, 'don't worry. I'll get you up when I wake, which will be about 7.30, OK?' I left him sitting there in reception. As I was walking down the corridor to my room, I could hear the receptionist laughing as Les went through his routines once more. I don't know where he got his stamina from.

The following morning I got dressed, packed and made my way to reception. All the others except Les were there waiting for me. 'Come on, Tommy!' they shouted. 'We'll be able to get a coffee at the airport.'

'Just a minute,' I replied. 'I have to give Les a call.'

I approached the reception desk and asked the receptionist, 'Could you give Mr Dawson a call, please?'

'Oh,' she replied, 'Mr Dawson's left. He left about an hour ago.'

I told all the guys and we set off for the airport to find Les. Fancy him getting there before we did! But Les was nowhere to be found at the airport. I went to the enquiry desk. 'Excuse me,' I said, 'we're looking for Mr Les Dawson. Could you put a message out over the Tannoy and tell him that we're in the café?'

'Oh, but he went out on the plane just before yours,' came the reply.

'Just a minute, are you telling me that he's already flown out?'

'Yes,' the guy at the desk answered, looking at me as if I was stupid.

'Don't mind me asking,' I continued, 'but where's the plane going that Mr Dawson is on?'

'Leeds.'

I did my best to stifle the laugh that was building up inside me. Les had caught the wrong plane. 'Thank you,' I said politely to the guy behind the counter and went off to tell the others.

Everyone roared with laughter. We could all imagine Les talking happily to people on the plane, and we could all imagine his face when he arrived in Leeds. It was a sketch he couldn't have written better himself. About two weeks later I saw him and, just like the great man he was, he made a joke about it. I asked him what had happened and he told me that he had never gone to bed at all that night, but had eventually just left for the airport. He said he was that drunk he hadn't realized he was getting on the wrong plane. It was only when he landed in Leeds that he realized what an idiot he had been. It took Les at least six months to live that one down!

Back home, a surprise phone call from Fox Studios in America made my ears prick up, and I immediately wondered if we were to be invited back to the USA for another season. 'Hello, is that Mr Cannon?' enquired a drawling voice John Wayne would have been jealous of.

'Yes,' I replied, wondering who it was and getting a little excited inside.

'Well, I represent the Laurel and Hardy Appreciation Society here at Fox Studios in America,' the voice continued.

'Really...' I didn't quite know what to say. What was this about?

'Well, Mr Cannon, I have some good news for you. Your partner and yourself have won the Laurel and Hardy Appreciation Society trophy for comedy!'

I was absolutely thunderstruck, and found it hard to speak. To think that they had even heard of Bobby and me at the famous Fox Studios, let alone awarded us a comedy trophy! My ego swelled in the silence.

'Are you still there?' said the voice.

'Er, yes,' I replied. 'I'm just a little shocked, that's all.'

'I understand,' he said. 'There have been only two other comedy acts presented with this trophy in the last 20 years – Dean Martin and Jerry Lewis and Abbot and Costello. So as you can appreciate, Mr Cannon, it's quite an honour.'

'Yes it is,' I stuttered, feeling very humble. 'Bobby and I are both *very* honoured.' I was now so excited that I wanted the guy to get off the phone so that I could telephone Bobby with the news.

'Don't mind me asking,' the man went on, 'but where will you put the trophy, Mr Cannon?'

'Oh,' I replied, my northern roots coming out, 'on the mantelpiece.'

'Mantelpiece? What's that?'

Of course, he was American and wouldn't understand me. 'It's a shelf over the fireplace,' I explained.

'Oh, I see,' he said. 'Don't you have a trophy room, Mr Cannon?'

'No I don't.' I started to feel rather small and insipid.

'So winning trophies is quite a new thing to you then?' he continued.

'I suppose so,' I replied nervously, as if I'd done something wrong.

'Well, if you don't mind me saying,' he said, 'the trophy may look out of place on your, as you say, "mantelpiece".'

'Well, I could put it in my window?' I was getting into the mood now, gleefully planning where we should place the trophy.

'No,' he said, 'I don't think that would be appropriate.'

'I've got a piano. Can I put it on that?' I offered.

The voice on the line was suddenly smothered with laughter. 'Well, Tommy,' I heard the man say, 'you can put it where you want, because there's no trophy and this is Jimmy Tarbuck and you've just been wound up!' The phone went dead.

I couldn't believe my ears. Tarby had got me! He was well known for winding people up and now he had added me to his list. I put the phone down and started to chuckle myself. I'd been really taken in. I haven't got him back yet, but some day I will.

Being on the end of a wind-up happens so much to us that it's almost becoming a vocation. In true show business tradition, it wasn't long after Jimmy's efforts that our audience in Torquay experienced something that could happen only once. Bobby and I were doing a piece called 'The Puppet Sketch', which involved a wall set up in the middle of the stage. The whole sketch was a wonderful idea that had been penned by Sid Green. He and his partner Dick Hills had written for Morecambe and Wise, and now Sid was writing for us with an understanding for comedy that remains unsurpassed.

The sketch was underway, and in full flow I moved behind the wall, only to gasp out loud. Freddy Starr was lying down behind the wall, hidden from view. This certainly wasn't in the script! We weren't even aware that he was in the resort. He was obviously up to no good and was about to pounce on us with some sort of trick.

Staring down at the heap on the floor, I couldn't decide what to do next, because it's impossible to tell how Freddy's mind is working. All I could do was laugh. Bobby looked at me oddly, because I was laughing when I shouldn't have been, and I did what all double acts do when they're in trouble: I signalled to him with my eyes. He came back behind the wall to see what the trouble was and stared down at Freddy. Now I was really worried, because Bobby can be as crazy as Freddy!

Suddenly Bobby kicked the wall down and there was Freddy in full view of the audience, curled up like a little baby on the floor. We both jumped on him and it became total mayhem. The audience was going wild, when suddenly I spotted Jim Davidson watching us from the wings. Bobby saw him too, jumped up and hauled him on stage and then there were four of us rolling around together.

The audience hadn't expected to see Bobby, Freddy Starr, Jim Davidson and myself all on stage at the same time. They cheered and clapped at the impromptu entertainment and when we eventually finished the show, we agreed that it had been a wonderfully unique night.

The next day we put our thinking caps on, wondering how we could get Freddy back. Having discovered that he was appearing at the same theatre on the Sunday of that week, Bobby and I decided to pay him an unannounced visit. When we got to the stage door there was a huge bouncer waiting. 'Sorry, Tommy and Bobby,' he said, 'but I can't let you in – Freddy's orders.'

We couldn't believe it. 'Well, we're going in whether you let us or not,' Bobby answered back, little Jack Russell type that he is.

'OK,' said the bouncer, 'but if Freddy sees you, tell him that you sneaked past me!'

Once we got inside we could hear Freddy on stage, so we crept into his dressing room, planning to jump on him when he came in. Then Bobby found a German helmet. 'Watch this, Tommy,' he said, and slipped out of the dressing room. I followed him to the side of the stage, and we waited until Freddy started singing a serious song. 'Watch!' Bobby whispered, and stepped out onto the stage.

The audience went wild, shouting, 'Rock on, Tommy!' Freddy just looked at Bobby, and Bobby stared back at him. 'That's how you do it, Freddy,' he said, and stepped back into the wings.

Freddy waited until the audience's excitement had died down, then he just looked at them and said with a slight stutter, 'Who was that?' The audience went wild again. Freddy had used his simple comic genius to top us, and he was the king at that. We met up afterwards and had a good laugh about the whole evening.

Bobby and I must be vulnerable to wind-ups, because it was only a short time afterwards that we found ourselves on a plane going to Rome in order to make a short film about Italian tomatoes. Our new agent had told us that it was a great opportunity to make a television advert about a very popular product on behalf of the European Tomato Growers Association. Sitting on the plane, we were feeling slightly suspicious. Why was the production company going to such lengths to make what seemed like a rather silly film? We considered the idea that it might be a wind-up, but dismissed the thought because of all the money the trip must have cost to arrange.

When we arrived at the airport no one came to meet us and we had to find our own way to the hotel. 'This trip is a right shambles!' I said to Bobby.

When we finally reached the hotel our suspicions were aroused once again as we met Esther Rantzen and her husband coming out of the reception area. They seemed taken aback to meet us too, but we all just dismissed it as a coincidence.

We were then ushered by a strange Italian into a local recording studio, where we spent the morning trying to tape a song. It was all sung in Italian, but we did our best, which was still pretty awful. They kept telling us that we weren't putting enough drama and emphasis into the song, and we didn't have the heart to tell them we didn't understand a word!

I have to admit to feeling pretty stupid that despite all this farcical evidence we didn't twig what was happening, not even when we were whisked off to the main market street in Rome and shown our costumes. Standing on the pavement as we got out of our car were the two biggest tomatoes you've ever seen. They were made of foam covered with bright red fabric and there were holes cut out for our faces and arms.

We were helped into these heavy costumes, but not before we had been made to replace our trousers with tights. We must have looked the funniest pair of idiots in the city, and passers-by either stared in disbelief or collapsed in laughter. One guy kept coming up and telling us that we didn't look like tomatoes. This constant interruption really began to annoy us after a while, but we still kept our calm on the outside.

Filming began and everything seemed to go wrong around us. The lighting caused problems, the music scripts were always wrong, and the director had a tantrum. Four hours later we were no nearer getting this farce 'in the can'. Bobby and I couldn't understand what was going on, but somehow we kept our cool. After all, we figured, we were being paid to do the job.

The director announced that he needed another tomato for a bigger shot and suddenly, from out of nowhere, another huge tomato-person appeared and started to chat to us between takes. A little later, just at the moment of greatest frustration, a little door in the third tomato opened and out popped a 'Gottcha' award! Noel Edmunds had been behind the whole escapade. Bobby and I were so filled with surprise and relief that we just jumped on him and bundled him to the ground. I don't know what the shoppers of Rome thought about seeing three huge tomatoes writhing around on the ground in the middle of their marketplace! We had said to Noel many years previously that we would never be taken in by him; we would always be able to sniff him out, we boasted. How wrong we were, and how glad we are that we were well and truly 'Gottcha'd!'

Being wound up is one thing; being cheated and robbed is quite another, and I shudder to think of the time when I caught the gambling bug. The only good thing about it was that it saved me from ever risking my money in the future. At the height of our success, when the money was flowing and the world was at my feet, I decided to buy a racehorse. I had never been interested in them before, so it probably just attracted me because it was something else to try. I paid £8,000, which isn't really a lot of money for a racehorse.

'I've bought a racer,' I told Bobby.

'How much have you paid for it?' he asked.

'Eight grand, and it's a beauty,' I told him, trying to sound knowledgeable about racehorses. 'I've called it Cannon's Way.'

Bobby looked at me. 'Eight grand! You must be crackers!' he said. 'You've bought a donkey!'

'Well, we'll see,' I replied, refusing to let my pride be dented. 'It's running next week, so why don't you have a bet on it?'

'You've no chance,' he replied. 'It's got no chance of winning.'

My horse entered the race the following week and to everybody's surprise, including mine, it won. I couldn't wait to tell Bobby. That night I almost ran into his dressing room. 'It's won!' I gloated. 'I told you!'

Bobby's mouth dropped open. 'You *are* joking?' he said.

'No,' I replied, 'and it's running this weekend. Are you having a bet now?'

'No,' he said, much to my surprise. 'That was a lucky win. You've no chance next time.'

My horse ran again, and won again. By this time the gambling bug had started to crawl into my soul. 'It's won again!' I screamed at Bobby. He just couldn't believe it. 'It's running again in a few days, are you going to have a bet this time?'

Once again Bobby refused. 'There's no way that it can win three times in a row,' he said. 'Blimey! You only paid £8,000 for it.'

It did win again. I began to feel my horse could never lose. It ran four straight wins and Bobby didn't bet on any of them. Then in the fifth race it lost. My trainer said that the horse had started to 'suck wind' and that it would be a good idea to sell it while it had a good track record.

I sold it for £8,000, the amount I had paid for it, but I had made £12,000 in winnings. This seemed to me an easy way to make money and I was hooked. The next horse I bought was called Cannon's Girl, and this time I paid £20,000. I presumed that because I had paid more than double what I had for my first horse, this one would make me a fortune. How wrong I was! It didn't win a single race. I eventually sold it for £3,000 and all the money I had previously made was gone.

It was during this time, about 1990–91, that I had just gone through my divorce from Margaret, and as everybody knows divorces are expensive. With my losses on the horses, money was in short supply. Hazel and I moved into a new home after going to the bank for a loan to raise the deposit, and we found ourselves looking at a future that seemed very bleak. At weekends we would stay at a hotel in London because we were mainly working down there, and one day I was reading the paper when an advertisement caught my eye. 'Exclusive Gambling,' it read, 'sincere partner required.'

I still had the gambling bug running around inside me, so the advertisement caught my interest even though I was low on money. I rang the telephone number listed in the advert and made myself known to the guy on the other end of the phone. He told me he was from Brighton and that I had made a good choice to become his partner. We got some sort of relationship going and he said he would be in touch. I put the phone down and thought no more about it.

A week later he phoned me up. 'Hi, Tommy,' he said, 'we've got a horse running this week and I want you to put £5,000 on it.'

'Sorry?' I gasped, nearly dropping the phone.

'Oh, it's OK,' he said, 'I was just seeing how much you would gamble on a horse if we had a sure winner.'

'Well,' I said, '£5,000, that's a lot of money. I don't think I could raise that sort of cash.' I knew I couldn't.

'Don't worry about it,' he said, 'I was only testing you. I'll ring you back later on in the week.'

True to his word, he rang back the following week. This time he said he had a horse and he wanted me to put £2,000 on it. I said OK, and somehow raised the money. Then I went to the bookie's and put the money down. My adrenaline was going through the roof. I was becoming addicted. I'll never forget the little bookmakers in Duke Street, London. They checked everything out because they obviously knew who I was and thought that somehow I'd got really good tips. They took the bet because the horse was running at very long odds. I stood there in the bookie's open mouthed as the horse romped home at odds of 10 to 1. I felt like crying, and went back to the hotel carrying £20,000 stuffed into every pocket available.

I thought I had found the goose that laid the golden egg, that life was going to be fine from now on and that all my money worries were over. 'George' phoned me again and said that he wanted a commission of 1 per cent. He would send a runner to collect the money. My orders were to put the money in an envelope with my room number on it and leave it behind the desk of the hotel. I did what I was instructed and never saw the guy. By this stage all sorts of suspicions should have been screaming at me, but they weren't – I was just too hooked on gambling. About two weeks later he rang me again and said that he had another horse. So we bet again and won, and after that we had a few more bets – nothing major, but they were still wins.

Bobby and I were touring in a play called *You'll Do For Me*, and we were in south Wales when Hazel told me that she was pregnant. I was over the moon. I couldn't believe that I was starting all over again with babies. My two girls had grown up, and now here I was going to be a dad again. I know that some people wouldn't like it, but for me it was magic news and gave me a new lease of life. I wouldn't have time to be old now!

That week 'George' rang me up again and said that he wanted me to put £15,000 on three horses, £5,000 on each. At first I said 'no way', but then I reasoned to myself that I was really just playing with the money because I'd won a few races. I was getting 'gamblers' logic'. So I put £15,000 on the horses and yes, you've guessed it, they all lost! The £15,000 was gone in a flash. During that time in south Wales, Hazel miscarried the baby and I think it was because of my excessive gambling. She must have been worried sick about our future, with a baby coming along and me gambling away everything we had.

Later on, when we got back home, 'George' phoned me again. This time he said that it was crazy the way we were sending money all over the country, and the best thing to do would be to open an account at the bookie's. To do this I would have to deposit £15,000 and then we could open an account. Like the fool I am, I agreed. I thought that everything would be all right and I could raise the money because I was already £10,000 in front from my previous winnings, and all I had to find was £5,000. I convinced myself that the last three horses which had lost were the first ones to spoil my chances and everything would change for the better now.

Off we went again, and yes, we lost again. Then for some strange reason we started to lose every time we bet – £10,000 here, £10,000 there, until eventually all the money I had given him plus my deposit had gone. I couldn't get myself out of the situation in which I now found myself. The more money I lost, the more I would try to chase my losses. I now owed that much money I didn't know what to do or who to turn to. I didn't tell Bobby about the mess I was in, and when I did tell him a few years later he was really hurt that I hadn't turned to him for help at the time.

I was getting suspicious about the fact that I kept losing, until one day 'George' said that he was coming to York, where I now lived, to see me. He turned out to be very well dressed and looked every inch the business-man. He was a likable fellow and the type of guy I felt I could trust. He told me that the reason he couldn't bet himself was that he had won such vast amounts of money on the horses the bookies wouldn't take his bets any more. Therefore he had to use people like me to do the betting and take a percentage of the winnings for himself. I'd heard about this sort of thing before, so I believed that it was all right – and of course we'd been winning until we'd hit this losing streak.

Despite his explanations, I continued to lose and my suspicions grew even more. I ended up losing about £30,000 and owing him about £50,000. After much heart-searching and discussions with Hazel, I phoned 'George' and told him that I wanted to stop. I didn't have any more money and I couldn't pay what I owed him.

I couldn't believe what happened next. The nice, amenable man who had met me in York suddenly turned into a different animal. He started to scream obscenities down the phone. 'Listen Cannon!' he shouted, 'Don't think you can f*****g walk away from me. You owe me the b****y money and I'm going to get it! I'll f*****g well send some guys up there and they'll break your f*****g legs, you b*****d! You'd better expect a f*****g visit soon!'

I had never heard so many swearwords in one sentence. During his threatening tirade I realized with heavy dread that I had been suckered and had unknowingly entered a violent and dangerous world. I had well and truly been taken for a ride. Some people never learn and I was one of them. I went to see a lawyer to find out what I could do in this situation. He was a wonderful man and made me feel at ease, for which I was grateful. The lawyer contacted an ex-policeman from Brighton who had turned private investigator, and asked him to find out what he could about 'George'. I gave him the phone number that I had been using and the address of 'George's' office. When the investigator checked the phone numbers they turned out to be public phone boxes. The address was fictitious.

'George' was simply the leader of a gang of guys who would place adverts in newspapers to trap gullible idiots like me, then they would get them into so much debt that they would give anything to get away from their erstwhile 'partners'. The investigator couldn't trace where they operated from, but found out that 'George's' father had been arrested for murder.

The investigator's advice to me was to back off and leave it alone, and certainly to forget about taking the matter to court. I reluctantly agreed. In another meeting with my lawyer I told him I had no intention of paying 'George' the £50,000 that I supposedly owed him. He said that if 'George' phoned me again, I was to tell him that I had seen my lawyer and that on his advice I wasn't giving him any more money and was going to the press to expose him. If he didn't ring, then it was best to let sleeping dogs lie.

Sure enough, though, 'George' soon phoned once more. I told him my intentions and he went ballistic. After about five minutes of listening to him screaming abuse, I quietly said, 'Listen George, it's up to you, but as far as I'm concerned I'm going to blow all this up in the press, because who knows, this may help to stop people gambling and getting into situations like the one I find myself in. Now, George, I'm going to give you a number I want you to ring and hopefully this can be sorted out.'

I gave him my lawyer's number and he put the phone down. Two days later my lawyer actually received a phone call from him. My lawyer was very civil but threatening. He told 'George' that if he didn't cooperate, his client would have no alternative but to go to the press and get the police involved. On the other hand, if he did cooperate and just walked away, then nothing more would be heard on the matter. 'George' agreed.

It was all so scary that for three months I slept with a shotgun under my bed. About a month after all this, Bobby and I got a booking at a place called Jenkins Bar in Brighton. I was petrified as thoughts of 'George' came flooding back. Luckily the booking got cancelled a week before we were due to appear. Boy, was I relieved!

CHAPTER FOURTEEN

THE WIND BENEATH OUR WINGS

Abraham Lincoln once commented that the best thing about the future is that it only comes one day at a time. Cannon and Ball have spent their past climbing the mountains and trudging the valleys in their journey through life together. Theirs is a story of two guys who accepted their destiny to make people laugh, but nearly lost it all to the seduction of show business. Bobby says, 'It's better to climb the mountains than ignore them, because that's the only way you get to see the view.' When Tommy is asked about his visions of the future, however, he's more hesitant to reply.

The future? Who knows what the future brings? Certainly in show business you never know what's around the corner. There's a great saying in the Bible: 'Don't worry about tomorrow, today has enough problems of its own.' We can't say what will happen next, but as far as today is concerned Bobby and I couldn't have it any better. I don't mean in terms of money, success and fame – we value more personal things now, especially when we see what others have to cope with.

Bobby and I were recently invited to the infamous Wormwood Scrubs, to entertain the inmates as well as talk about our lives in show business. It was quite an eye-opener for us as we were ushered through several metal doors into an area that they used for body searches. Having been frisked and found safe, we were led into the main block on the way to the community hall. As we walked past row upon row of cell doors, each with a tiny observation hole, we began to imagine how difficult life in the Scrubs must be. Despite the jolly chat from the wardens, the place had a foreboding atmosphere.

Reaching the hall, we walked onto the platform area and were immediately cheered by about 100 men who had all sat patiently waiting for our arrival. Bobby and I felt privileged to be there, because we felt sad for some of these guys, particularly the youngest ones, who were 'banged up' in this old building. If the Inland Revenue investigation had gone against us, I reflected, we might actually have been in here ourselves.

We were pleased at the opportunity to bring a little bit of fun and hope into these men's lives, whatever wrong they had done. Bobby's eyes were twinkling with naughtiness and I could see that he was in a rebellious mood. He started to break the ice with a few gags and I noticed a guy in the second row with a mohican haircut and earrings. I hoped Bobby wouldn't pick on this really tough-looking guy, but that's exactly what he did, proceeding to take the mickey out of him, which his friends found really amusing.

Ironically, our house had been burgled three days previously and several things had been stolen, so when I started to speak I asked the guys whether they knew who'd done it and where my possessions had gone. That got another big laugh.

We chatted for about 40 minutes, explaining how our lives had another side to the glamour portrayed on TV and describing some of the difficulties we had been through. We succeeded in making them laugh, but finished by encouraging them to believe that there is always a way through the hard times. Once the final applause had died down, we noticed that as they were led back to their cells some of these hardened criminals had tears in their eyes. I suppose they felt they could relate to some of the things we said, and maybe some of them were even able to change their ways afterwards.

As we stood around waiting to be shown the way out, I noticed that all the prisoners had been escorted away apart from some wearing black armbands. These men began to bring trays of tea and biscuits around, and I asked one of the warders the meaning of the armbands. I listened intently while he explained that these were the 'lifers' who had special privileges because of the heavy sentences they bore. In other words, these were the most dangerous men in the prison.

When I looked up, there was the guy with the mohican haircut and earrings, complete with tray, offering tea and biscuits to some other guys across the room! The shock of being so close to a 'lifer' caused my bottom to twitch and my mouth to crease up in an obviously nervous smile as he looked across in our direction. My heart jumped a beat or two when he actually started to walk towards us, and I remembered how Bobby had poked fun at him.

I did a nonchalant sideways walk towards Bobby and whispered in his ear. 'He's on his way over!' I hissed.

'Who?' asked Bobby in bewilderment.

'That hard nut you messed with!' I screeched between clenched teeth.

Mr Mohican was walking over to us with the most serious face imaginable. 'This is it!' I thought, scenes from countless films where the prisoner whips out a home-made knife smuggled from the workshop whirling round in my head.

We turned to meet him as he approached, and when he was just a few steps away he suddenly burst out laughing. 'That was great, man!' he said as he slapped me on the back.

'You didn't mind Bobby ribbing you, then?' I asked tentatively.

'No, I loved every minute of it, and you've given the guys in here something to think about too,' he replied.

Starting to relax, I stood and talked to him for a while and he told me that he had shot his friend over an argument about drugs. I found myself feeling sorry for him. One brief moment, and two lives were completely destroyed. The memory of him stayed vividly with me for some time and I still think about how he's doing. The prison audience may have been our smallest, but it was certainly one of the most worthwhile and helped us appreciate the value of our own lives more.

We still get a thrill from topping bills in theatres, which is quite an achievement after so long, but it's not the only thing we live for now. We don't feel any desperation to get back on TV because its style of comedy has changed – which in some ways is probably a good thing. Comedy has to change or it wouldn't move on. It might not always be for the better in every detail, but it has to progress nevertheless. There are a lot of good young comics coming through, and whether we like them or not, they are the future of comedy.

Of course, if the right TV vehicle came along we would gladly be part of it, but as we still do good business in summer seasons and pantomimes, we're happy and don't take our continued popularity for granted. Playing to capacity houses, our last season in Blackpool broke even more box-office records. Plenty of our friends are no longer working and we're honoured that our audience still laughs at the funny little man and the straight guy. In fact, the act just seems to be getting stronger – even if Bobby and I are getting slower because of our age.

When I first met Bobby he was only 19 years old, weighed eight stone, had a head full of hair and was full of energy. Now he weighs 11 stone and his hair is thinning, but he still has that energy. I'm no better: when I met Bobby I had a head full of hair too, but now I'm as bald as a coot, which Bobby never stops reminding me about. It's good to grow old together, because we've been through so many things together. People are right when they compare our relationship to a marriage, and I'm proud of the fact that two guys can have such an extremely close friendship, an unusual phenomenon these days. British fellas are very reserved and don't make friends easily, especially close friendships which are strong enough to lean on at all times. I'm so grateful for the time we've been given together, and I cherish each moment we have now. It's still my ambition to walk on stage together when we've both reached 70. That would be fantastic for me.

My marriage to Hazel is all that I ever dreamed it would be, and more, and we have great kids. Every time I look at my family I realize just how much I'm blessed. I have to thank Hazel with all my heart for her patience, because sometimes I'm difficult to live with. I love them all tremendously and I thank the Lord that my life has worked out to be so great.

Life off stage keeps me busy, as I'm not one for sitting around. I set up a company called Millennium Organic two years ago as a hobby and it has turned into quite a nice little business, which Hazel now runs. When I'm at home I look and feel like a right 'Farmer Jones' and I love to work on the land with all types of specialist crops. My daughter Janette is a hospital receptionist and she has given me three wonderful grandchildren, with my eldest grandson Ben working on the farm in the school holidays. My other daughter Julie has an interesting job as a hotel manager just round the corner from where I live, so I'm lucky enough to see her most days.

My middle grandson Alex wants to do everything at once. He wants to dance, sing, play drums, act – he wants it all, but luckily he has plenty of time. My youngest grandson is Matty. We don't know yet how he'll turn out – he's just a wild kid with the most mischievous eyes I've ever seen. I love all three of them and they are near and dear to my heart.

Hazel works hard for our organic business as well as looking after our children. Our daughter Kelly is at stage school and I understand she's a very good pupil. Zoë, who's a little younger, is coming along very nicely too and also wants to go to stage school when she's old enough. 'Don't put your daughter on the stage, Mrs Worthington,' I hear you hum! Well, I never thought that I'd have two girls who would want to follow me into show business. I suppose with Hazel having been a dancer and myself a comic, what could I expect? Funnily enough, it's a bit of a nightmare for me, maybe because I

234

know all the pitfalls so well! If that's their choice, however, I'll be behind them all the way.

My only son Luke is a smashing little chap. I love him to bits, just as I love all my kids. I'd like him to be an aspiring sportsman, and I suppose all fathers want their sons to achieve the things they didn't get to do themselves. Of course, he might be like Bobby and turn out to have two left feet. Whatever he becomes – and certainly if he's as talented as Bobby – then I'll be very pleased.

I'm grateful that I can still sing my heart out on stage, and often reminisce about those days I spent crooning behind the hospital wall. Something I never believed would come true has happened, and some of my most enjoyable moments on stage are the songs. It's even better when Bobby doesn't interrupt me!

The songs have changed over the years, but amongst my favourites 'Wind Beneath My Wings' still stands as one of the best songs ever written. We'd become bored using 'He Ain't Heavy, He's My Brother' to close the act after many years and we needed a replacement. I first heard 'Wind Beneath My Wings' on an American album, and not long afterwards Tony Christie was singing it. I adopted it for our act and before long it was a big hit around the world. Everyone was singing it after that, but it's still special for us. How could I have known that many years later the lyrics would have an even greater significance in my life?

For at the end of the day, it's not only Bobby's past that I share, it's his future too. We both have a strong faith in God now, which we know will take us through anything. No verse could be truer for me than the one that says, 'Even if I go through the deepest darkness, I will not be afraid, Lord, for you are with me.' I've seen this proved again and again in our lives. Whatever happens, the future is bright!

The arrival of the year 2000 saw Cannon and Ball celebrate 37 years together as a double act, a long time in anyone's estimation. To live in each other's pockets for such an extended time is no mean feat and they obviously still enjoy each other's company enormously, a fact that Bobby attributes to the effect their Christian faith has had on their lives. Bobby was never one to be 'religious', and he's still far from being 'just a churchgoer'. Bobby is someone who tries to take his faith out from the church and put it into practice, and this has a great effect on how he views the future.

The future? I never look at it. I only think about today, because as a Christian I believe that the future belongs to God. That's quite a relief, really – to know that someone else is ultimately in control. I look around today at what I have and still see God working. Tommy and I have achieved heights that very few people reach. We have also plummeted to depths that would have destroyed many, but I found it was the depths that had the greatest effect on my life. When I thought I had nowhere to turn, I found that God was there. He gave me an inner strength, and I grew stronger as a whole person. I now look at everything as a blessing, something that I haven't earned and maybe don't deserve.

Yvonne is my greatest blessing. She was there for me when I was stumbling around in the darkness. She was there to hold my hand, and she stood quietly as I rampaged through drink and adultery, waiting for me. She loves with an unconditional love and I've learned to love her in the same way. My love for Yvonne grows all the time, and each day I see something new in her.

My children are also a blessing to me. Robert my eldest, Darren my middle boy and Joanne my 'baby' fill my heart with love every time I see them. Children are one of God's greatest blessings – they're such bundles of potential. Robert and Darren have followed me into the business and are a double act themselves. They have both been professional for 10 years and have worked hard refining their act. They are starting to become popular in clubs and theatres around the country. When I see them I feel very proud and sometimes (but not often!) I yearn for the days when Tommy and I had just started out.

Joanne is going to college at the moment to help her achieve her ambition to become an author, and I'm sure she'll succeed. I'm very proud of the way she has made a great mother to my grandchildren and a great wife to her husband. Her life revolves around her kids and sometimes when I see the love emanating from them it thrills me to have her as a daughter.

Between them, my children have given me six grand-children and each one of them has a character of their own. There's Ben, Christian, Samuel, Jack, Robert and my only granddaughter to date, Bethany. I constantly nag the kids to give me more, on the off-chance that I may get another granddaughter! Yes, I've certainly been blessed with my family.

I also count it a blessing to enjoy the health, opportunity and popularity to continue working. During a recent season at The Grand Theatre in Blackpool, I was worried that my age was starting to affect my performance. I've always been deaf in one ear and, because my left ear was the strongest, I always stood on Tommy's right side. That way I could be sure of making contact with him. Increasingly, however, I found that I couldn't hear the audience laughing as much as I should have been able to, and used to come off stage thinking we had struggled.

I would turn to Tommy and say, 'We struggled then, didn't we?'

Tommy would look at me and shake his head. 'We stormed 'em! You want to get that ear seen to!'

Then Yvonne said she needed some new reading glasses, and just around the corner from the house we had rented for the season was an optician's. One day we were passing the shop and Yvonne decided to pop in to get her glasses. I don't know if she planned it, but right next door to the optician's was a hearing aid shop.

'While I'm getting my glasses,' Yvonne said to me, 'why don't you go and see about getting a deaf aid?'

I looked at her in horror. 'A deaf aid?' I said. 'I'm a comedian!'

'What's being a comedian got to do with being deaf?' she replied, looking at me as if I'd gone crazy.

'Yvonne,' I said, getting exasperated, 'I'm not that deaf!'

'You must be joking,' she replied. 'When we have the TV on people six streets away know what channel we're watching!'

'It's not that bad,' I said defensively. 'Besides, I'd look stupid with a deaf aid sticking out of my ear.'

'You don't need a deaf aid to do *that*,' she told me, 'and besides, look in the window – they do those invisible ones.'

'Well, they must work because I can't see them,' I replied, trying to make light of a situation I knew I was losing.

'Look,' she said, 'just go and see. It can't do any harm.'

So I conceded and went into the shop. The guy in there was very nice and I asked him if I could just take a look at his deaf aids. He told me that I would have to take a hearing test first, which I did. The results weren't terrific. I had 85 per cent hearing loss in my right ear and he told me that my left ear was taking all the strain, so later on in life I would lose my hearing in that one too because it was doing all the work. This convinced me pretty fast, so I decided to have a hearing aid after all. He told me it would be a couple of weeks before I could have it, because he had to take a mould of my ear, which would be sent away to be made into the aid. This was agreed and Yvonne and I went away happy – Yvonne more than me, because she would no longer have to watch TV with her fingers in her ears.

Eventually my hearing aid arrived and I tried it on. It was wonderful being able to hear so many things that I'd missed before. It fitted snugly right down inside my ear and all that showed was a tiny aerial which looked like a hair. It was marvellous and that night I went to the theatre wearing my new equipment, enjoying the sound of the seagulls. When I showed Tommy my new deaf aid he quipped, 'I won't be able to talk behind your back any more then!' Laughing, he then said he was glad that I would be able to hear how well we were doing with the audience, instead of him having to reassure me all the time.

We went on stage and it was even better than I had anticipated. For the first time in years I could actually hear the audience laughing properly. I turned to Tommy and whispered, 'Hey, we're not bad, are we?'

ROCK ON, TOMMY!

It was so good and I was so excited, that I decided to tell the audience about my new deaf aid. How stupid can you be? I'd bought an invisible hearing aid so that it couldn't be seen and now I was telling 1,000 people about it! Don't ask me why, but I was just so proud. I didn't make a big thing about it, I just told them that I was a little bit deaf and that I'd bought a new hearing aid that day.

Everything was going OK until I started sweating under the stage lights. My hearing aid wasn't feeling as snug as it had done earlier, and then suddenly I started to hear a whistling sound. 'Oh no,' I thought to myself, 'my hearing aid is feeding back!' As I tried adjusting the earpiece I had flashbacks of my father who'd had a hearing aid that would whistle – and now mine was doing it.

The audience started to laugh and the more they laughed the more I panicked. I thought they could hear the whistling through the sound system. I nonchalantly wiggled the hearing aid a bit more, but this only seemed to make things worse. The whistling became louder and the audience laughed even more. As I was squirming in embarrassment I noticed a movement just to the left of me. I turned round – and caught Tommy with his mouth pursed. It hadn't been my hearing aid at all, but Tommy whistling! The audience was loving it and Tommy broke out into a huge grin, knowing that he'd got away with a clever trick. Everyone clapped, obviously pleased to see such warmth between the two of us. Little did they know that they would never have seen that a few years previously.

It's not easy to make and keep true friends in this business, probably because we're always moving around too much, but I have been lucky enough to have made some friends and one of these is a man named Keith Chadwick. I met Keith at a church dinner and he became one of my closest friends. He's a very knowledgeable man and a little eccentric, which I like. We spend many hours together discussing the world and silly things like that, and after all the tribulations I've been through he's one of the few men that I can really trust. He's a good friend to me and one that I cherish and value as an important part of my journey through life.

Comedy is a strange profession to pick. The song gets it right: 'There's no business like show business.' It can be great and it can be bad. The good times are when an audience roars with laughter and you know that for a short while they have forgotten their everyday problems. The bad times are when they don't laugh and you know you're being judged for trying to take away their troubles with a smile. People sometimes ask whether I'm a comedian or a comic, and is there any difference? Well, yes there is. A comedian is a man who tells funny stories and a comic is a funny man. Which am I? That's for you to decide.

Of course, it's Tommy who has been my greatest friend and partner, and despite the gag with the stripper backfiring, he still tries to shock me on stage. In recent years I used to sing a song called 'Little Donkey' and it got on everybody's nerves, especially Tommy's, but that only made me sing it all the more. One night I was singing this song when the audience started laughing unexpectedly loudly. I looked behind me and there was Tommy, holding onto a real donkey!

I couldn't believe my eyes. It might not sound like much, but when you consider the amount of work

Tommy went through to pull off this stunt, it was a pretty ingenious thing, really. He hired the donkey from a local sanctuary, brought it to the theatre, sneaked it into a dressing room which was one flight of stairs below the stage, fed it carrots all night to keep it quiet, then walked it up the stairs to bring it on stage.

The sight of the donkey and me gawping at it with my mouth wide open brought the house down. The donkey had a good time too, because the entire cast did nothing but pet and pamper him all night. I loved the idea of Tommy's trick and was so taken with the donkey that when Yvonne and I moved to a farm in 1995, I bought myself a donkey named Jemima. She was just like the ones that you see at the seaside, complete with straw hat and holes for the ears. She was a beautiful thing and would try to get into the house to see me. When I sat outside she would wander over and put her head on my shoulder, breathing into my ear. Yvonne said that Jemima was sick and was probably in love with me. I think Yvonne was only jealous, actually.

The tricks that Tommy plays on me are great fun and I enjoy the sense of naughtiness that exists between us. One of the things that I admire greatly about Tommy is that when I became a Christian he didn't turn against me or criticize my failings. He understood that my faith was everything to me and never tried to convince me of anything else. One of the greatest moments of my life was that after seven years of praying for Tommy he finally gave his life to God. This was one of the happiest days I've ever had, and after an experience like that show business seemed a very pale comparison.

It wasn't long after Tommy became a Christian that we were approached by the producer of my original gospel tour with the proposal that we present 'The Cannon and Ball Gospel Show'. The idea was that we would bring all the comedy, song, laughter and chat together to form one of the most spectacular shows that had toured for a very long time.

As the biggest show out on the road at that time, we carried everything on an articulated truck, with a separate sleeping bus to accommodate the nine crew and drivers. It was certainly one of the most expensive tours to produce, but it turned out to be one of the most successful too. We did 47 gigs across the nation, including dates in Ireland. It was such an unusual event that the show appeared on two specially made TV documentaries, and when it was finally released the video was one of the biggest sellers of its kind. It was such fun to do that going back to the usual routine of summer seasons and panto was the biggest professional anticlimax I'd ever experienced. So many amazing things happened on the tour that I can only save it for another book!

All good things come to an end, of course, and the show finished ready for us to go straight back into pantomime. Having been surrounded during the whole tour by people with whom we had a real comradeship and a special love for, it was now back to just Tommy and me. At the end of the day, it's always just the two of us – but Tommy is a man I'm so honoured to have as a partner, and I hope we continue to make people laugh for many years to come. Thanks for being there, Tommy.

I hope that I don't appear boastful, but I'm proud that two welders from Oldham have stayed together for so long, faced all types of highs and lows and yet are still standing! I do believe with all my heart that God had a big hand in our life journey. Having everything made us arrogant and self-centred; losing it all made us humble and happier. We believe that no matter what we face in life we can learn from it, and it can make us better people. Not only do we believe this, we hope that we've proved it too!